Untold Miracles
An Undeniable Memoir of Faith

Velma Palmer Ph.D

authorHOUSE®

AuthorHouse™
1663 Liberty Drive
Bloomington, IN 47403
www.authorhouse.com
Phone: 1-800-839-8640

Published by AuthorHouse   1/11/2013

ISBN: 978-1-4772-8524-4 (sc)
ISBN: 978-1-4772-8522-0 (dj)
ISBN: 978-1-4772-8523-7 (e)

Library of Congress Control Number: 2012921825

Dedication

It is with great pleasure that I dedicate this book to my children, Antoinette, Ricardo and Allison and to my husband, Matthew Palmer, who has been my rock, prayer partner, companion, and best friend.

For the Lord your God will bless you in all your harvest and in all the work of your hands and your joy will be complete. (Deuteronomy 16:15)

Special Note

Trust in the Lord with all thine heart and lean not to your own understanding, in all thy way acknowledge Him and he shall direct thy path. (Proverbs 3: 5-6)

This testimony is a message of struggle, hope, faith, courage and determination of Dr. Velma Palmer the author of this book, *Untold Miracles*. It conveys a message of powerful trust in God, knowing that regardless of one's situation, God will make negative experiences into positive lessons that can be shared with others.

Many events that occurred in the walk of life by the author will inspire your faith, expand your perception of the physical world and enrich your spiritual beliefs. You will know that all things are possible.

Contents

Foreword

I have known Dr. Palmer for over fifty years, and there are dozens of things that come to mind that could be used to describe her. However, there are certain words that if you know her, will not escape your attention—even in a glancing way. Dr. Palmer is hardworking, progressive, warm-hearted, generous, civic minded, family oriented, very religious, and a great writer. By the way the list is by no means exhausted. In the interest of time, I chose the above qualities.

A very long time ago Dr. Palmer decided to become a teacher—a better choice could not have been made—and I am reminded here of the poem, "The Road Not Taken" by Robert Frost. Dr. Palmer's caring mind and motherly instincts have propelled her further and further into the field of education. Hundreds of kids have learned how to become serious learners—and life-long learners for that matter, because they were blessed to have a caring teacher: Dr. Palmer

While she was dedicating her life to teaching others, she also found time to become more qualified. Over the years she has attended many schools so that she could learn how best to appeal to the young. As a warm-hearted person she has appealed to the young as well as the old. She is never too busy to offer a kind word to those who have fallen on hard times, the sick, the broken hearted, and simply those who need to hear a kind word.

Her generosity, and civic-mindedness know no bounds—she has given to so many causes they are too numerous to mention here. As a matter of fact those who know her know that she will not say no to their inquiries. As an upstanding member of the community (South Florida), she is a solidly involved in community affairs--through political, educational, and religious ties.

Dr. Palmer is very devoted to her church and she plays an active role in the church. A more religious person I am yet to see. Her religious devotion has guided her life as well as the lives of other members of her family. Praying is what she does daily. She likes to remind others that they should pray also.

Lastly, Dr. Palmer who is an avid reader is a prolific writer. This is clearly evident in her recent book *Untold Miracles.* In my humble opinion, if you are education-oriented, a community leader, a general reader or simply a lay person this book is a must read. It is insightful, full of wisdom, and teaches more than you would ordinarily see in comparable books. Thank you Dr. Palmer, your work will go a long way in opening minds as well as hearts.

Lloyd Brown

Introduction

Dr. Velma Palmer and her family relocated from Jamaica to Miami in the summer of 1985. There was an immediate turn of events in their lives and the description for these challenges and triumphs can only be described as miracles. Although everything seem to be unusual, her faith in God kept the family together as they experienced deliverance, healing, and power.

On arrival at Miami International Airport, her son's teddy bear who he considered his "Brother" was torn from his arms and thrown in a garbage bin by an immigration officer at the first check point. The officers were on the prowl for illegal substances so her son paid the price, although they had only basic necessities. The shock, hurt, and fear led to a total disaster. Within hours in Miami, Rick had wandered away from their new home determined to rescue "Brother" from his demise. The world around them ceased to exist. The panic went out with a cry, "We must find him! He does not know anyone, not even a phone number or an address!"

Within months the children tried to settle in school and were faced with major obstacles as well as bullying. They were not black enough in one case and not white enough in another case. They were considered misfits, which created major difficulties for them.

Ann, Rick, and Alli beamed with joy as they as they prepared for their first trip to the beach. Ann, the oldest went out in the ocean with her friends and within a short time she was declared dead by the paramedics; a victim of drowning. After a second testing was done, the family was informed that a weak pulse was detected and it would take a miracle for her to pull through. Ann's near death experience at Crandon Park Beach landed her in a coma for weeks as the doctors prepared the family for the worse. She beat all odds when she awoke from her coma, conscious of her surroundings, and had all her faculties intact. The doctors and the other medical staff declared that this must be a miracle.

Three major accidents followed, all involving her husband. Although the doctors' prognoses of Matthew were grim, he was delivered and healed completely. The events could be summarized by saying:

And we know that all things work together for the good of them that love God, to them who are called according to his purpose. (Romans 8:28)

Struggles

Life struggles blow at my door without regard
for race, age, physical beauty or strength.
How could you visit without an invitation?
I thought with fear!

I wish you had disappeared before you came.
Then a whisper came- if you can't appreciate me -
then you are stuck with me.
I pretended to stare, giving a deaf ear,
the pages of life began to reel,
but I'm determine to gain.

How often do we encounter this uninvited monster
along our journey?
We sometimes groan, sigh, ignore, pretend,
As we keep making strides.
Hold on to the helm and never give up.
Victory will gleam somewhere along the shores.

By Dr. Velma Palmer

Chapter 1
Untold Miracles

><><

But my God shall supply all your need according to his
riches in glory by Christ Jesus. (Philippians 4:19)

Mountains are the best description I could find to outline my life and the way God has allowed me to climb these rocky steps, and at times sloping areas in my life. My life began in Highgate, Saint Mary, Jamaica when my young mother, Ivy gave birth to me, a brown curly-haired baby girl that she named Velma Brown. It was a time of uncertainty and disappointment because Ivy's dreams of becoming a teacher became shadowed knowing that her gears had to be shifted to meet the needs of her new baby. Being a single mother in a new town away from family would make it difficult for her to raise a child as well as continue working. To complicate this matter, my father who was a bus conductor was rarely around because his job took him to various parishes in Jamaica.

Within months my young mother had to make a decision, "Ah! I will take my baby to Mama," she muttered, "that's the best thing right now." She packed our bags and boarded a bus with me and headed for Hartland her birthplace; this was another rural district within the parish of St. Mary. My mother was determined for the village to raise me. It was customary for neighbors and communities to be supportive of children and families, by addressing the child's well-being and needs during their upbringing. This method of raising children was considered shared responsibility, and children were fully aware that parenting was not confined to their individual parents only. As a result children had to obey and respect adults who were of no relation to them.

The major economy in Highgate was farming. There were no factories or companies. The prominent professions of the community were teaching, nursing or law enforcement. Finding employment, which was scarce, meant that people had to work on the farm cultivating numerous types of crops or being employed in housekeeping. Most people had limited resources so they were unable to afford college or trade schools for their children. They also maintained their family by cultivating their crops and selling them to exporters as well as the city market.

Mama and Papa were delighted to meet me, their only granddaughter, for the first time at the tender age of six months old. The household also consisted of my oldest brother, two uncles, one aunt--all were attending school. Growing up in a large extended family was a blessing as well as a curse sometimes. I was the youngest and the only granddaughter in the household, which I used to my advantage many times. I considered myself pampered by all the family members and both sides used this to their advantage. I was a scapegoat out of punishment for the boys as well as out of many of their chores. They would prepare me to support their stories with all kinds of references, such as their activities and locations during certain events. My reward from them was outstanding!

According to my aunt, as a result of my curly hair that had a striking resemblance of the picture "Betty" on the condensed milk can, I was nicknamed "Betty". A term of endearment, I was called Betty by everyone except my mother. My mom showed her resentment to the name by refusing to call me Betty. I didn't understand the reason for this; it would become a source for a lot of problems later in life. There were no explanations or discussions as to why and this affected me in numerous ways. I wanted my mother to call me Betty just as all the other members of the family. This may have been one factor that led me to feel unloved by my mother throughout my childhood. I fought with the unanswered question- *what is in a name?* There was a constant battle that raged within my heart. I carried a huge burden because there were no answers to my questions. I even inquired from my father if I were her step-daughter. I discerned how shocked he was but he calmly said, "No, not at all." My investigations have not unearthed any reasons for this rejection, so I am the first to confess that I do not know. I am blessed to have found strength in this song to deal with my lifelong problem.

Sometimes I'm discouraged
My load's hard to bear
And I feel myself stumble
'Neath my load of care
Then I ask Him this question
Oh my Lord, how long?
Then I hear His voice

Whisper, whisper, whisper
He carry me through

Oh how I need Jesus to carry me through
Along Life's journey
Yes you need him too
And when you're in trouble
Don't know what to do
Just Call on Jesus, Jesus, Jesus
He'll carry you trough

When storm are raging
And the high billows rolls
When sad winds of sorrow
Sweep over my soul
Then I reach for my refuge.
My safe hiding place
And I know that he'll
Keep me, keep me, keep me
In his wonderful grace.

My emotions had escalated to new heights especially when my grandmother (Mama) sent me to my parents for the summer holidays. In Hartland and Kingston my family called me Betty however, my mother refused to call me by any other name than Velma. As the years went by, all my focus and actions were intended to resolve my fears of being unaccepted by my mother. I knew that it is God who kept me through this storm. My sense of rejection haunted me and without His presence it would have been catastrophic.

Although my parents lived in Kingston, the big city, I was desperate to return to Hartland even before the summer ended, to continue my way of life at all costs. One theory concerning my actions can be linked to me being totally bonded to my grandparents at an early age. My mother may have felt some resentment from me at times due to this bonding. My father was an easy-going man who did not believe that children should be punished for their infractions. My mother was the total opposite. She was known as a strong disciplinarian. I hid my sense of distress from Mama and Papa carefully because it would have affected their relationship with my mother.

I had a sense of reaching the stars at an early age and it was known by almost everyone who met me. It was evident that I was a leader and I demonstrated it in my everyday life. I was always teaching, instructing, and guiding someone during my childhood. My parents supported me financially while I was living with my grandparents. My dad was my favorite; we both looked alike, and I was considered his favorite as well. My name was echoed by my entire family due to my level of intelligence and achievements I made at an early age. There were no doubts, they were extremely proud of me. Papa would share some of my abilities and achievements with his friends and how proud he was that both of us worked out complicated problems that affected people's daily lives.

Geography and politics were his favorites. What conversations we had! He constantly informed me about world affairs and its long-term effects. He instructed me to read sections of the newspaper and share my understanding. I developed a love for different forms of communication and it has impacted my writing and communication skills throughout my life.

My perception of my mother's rejection was always visible even to other family members as well as family friends. She praised my siblings for their achievements but ignored mine although my successes were above theirs in most cases. There were times when family members came to my defense by saying how could you forget Betty's award or her good grades. During those battles I was hurt, crushed to the point that I cried for relief. Numerous times Papa would chastise my mother in my presence for treating me in this manner. Mama would join in by saying, "I just can't understand this; she is your child just like the others." One of her favorite customs was to criticize me openly in public for any trivial thing. I was terrified when this happened because it was almost impossible to overcome the embarrassment. It took such a toll on me that I did not want to be in her presence at times because I felt out of place. After many years of a feeling the sense of *rejection* by my mother, I was convinced that if I pushed myself to the highest levels in education, my successes would change my circumstances. Instead, it only increased my frustration as well as my doubts. My experiences taught me that external achievements will never compensate for your internal problems. I developed a strong bond with my aunts and uncles and they have always embraced me as their baby sister. Whenever I wanted money, clothes or shoes I'd send messages to them in the United States, and they rarely denied my request. This was difficult for my mom; she would always say that, "The family let you have your own way by spoiling you."

> *For whom the LORD loveth he correcteth; even as a*
> *father the son in whom he delighteth. (Proverbs 3:12)*

My Mom returned home to Hartland a few years later to live and I was miserable. Her rules were clear and I was expected to be the model child that she envisioned. She was convinced that her parents were lax with their discipline, so she was going to correct my behavior. Within weeks she began teaching pre-school students at a center within the community. I was one of her students who was always in trouble.

Having my mother as my teacher was devastating; I felt like my freedom was plucked from under my feet. She expected me to be the best in academic achievements and excellent behavior, and I resented it. In one of my times-out for my infractions, I rebelled and I stuck two fruit seeds in my ear. The doctor's office was miles away and she was really mad with me for doing it. There were no clinics or hospital in this small district and there was no form of transportation at that time of day. In her desperation to find medical assistance she hurried home hoping that she would walk as fast as she could before the doctor departed for the day. On her way she saw a parent who inquired why she had left school so early. A short explanation led the parent to seek permission to intervene. This parent comforted me and asked me to remain calm while she used a bobby pin and removed the seeds from my ear.

Shortly after this incident I entered public school and I loved my new teacher. Secretly, I was hoping that my mom would return to Kingston. Her stay was much longer than I had anticipated but finally, my dad informed her that his job had put him in a more stable position and so he was better able to take care of the family. I was elated when my mom relocated from Hartland to Kingston. I did not care where they were going. All I wanted was to regain my freedom. I felt like I was caught up in two worlds and I loved one and hated the other. I loved to roam the bushes with the other children although they had to take turns lifting me up or setting me on a pony because I was unable to manage on my own.

As I grew, I gained strength and peace through songs and scripture verses that I studied in church. They had deep meaning to my life although I did not fully understand the extent. The more I read and repeated Psalm 27, I was convinced that it addressed my concerns, my inner being, and it gave me assurance and comfort especially at nights when the script began to roll in my mind:

The Lord is my light and my salvation; whom shall I fear?
The Lord is the strength of my life; of whom shall I be afraid?...Hear, O Lord, when I cry with my voice:
have mercy also upon me, and answer me...
When my father and my mother forsake
me, then the Lord will take me up...
Wait on the Lord; be of good courage,
And He shall strengthen your heart;
Wait, I say, on the Lord! (Psalm 27:1,7,10,14)

As I got older I excelled in school and in just about everything that I did. Walking a few miles from Hartland to Donnington All-Age School daily was exciting. My friends and I picked fruits, played games, played in the nearby river and ran to class by nine o'clock. School began with a song and a prayer and ended with "The Lord's Prayer" and a closing song. We were anxious to play as we ran home to do our chores before it got dark. Happy voices chimed in at the end of the day by singing:

Now the day is over,
Night is drawing nigh,
Shadows of the evening
Steal across the sky.

Now the darkness gathers,
Stars begin to peep,
Birds, and beasts and flowers
Soon will be asleep.

Jesus, give the weary
Calm and sweet repose;
With Thy tenderest blessing
May mine eyelids close.

Recess twice per day was a delight. I engaged in numerous games, ate my favorite snacks, and conversed with my friends. I raised money sometimes from my peers as payments for solving some of their mathematical problems so this placed me in the smart league. My teachers praised me constantly for my understanding and accomplishment in class and in my yearly examinations. I was a shining star throughout my school. Agricultural

Science and sewing were stressed as part of the curriculum and I had lots of fun learning them because it was applicable in my everyday life.

Mama prepared our homemade lunches daily and expected one of the boys to be responsible for it. In her absence they insisted that I take the lunch to school. One day I put an end to it by hiding the lunch bag on a grassy hill; ants turned it into an ant pile and we were all left without lunch. They realized that they were not going to be my 'boss' any time soon. We hid the incident from the adults, knowing there would be consequences and things went back to normal.

My physical state was also examined daily at school and on at home. I was expected to return from school with my navy-blue uniform looking like it had just left the ironing board and my black shoes still shining although I walked along the dusty road home. Sometimes, I had to give an account of my activities due to the state of my clothes. Secretly, I accompanied my friends on their quest for fruits and sugar cane from several properties along the way. We loved to feast on them as if we were starving but in truth our property had abundance for us to eat. Rainy days were exciting because the rules were less strict both at home and at school and I loved it. The years that I spent at Donnington All-Age School has created a lasting memory that I will always cherish.

My grandparents were well-respected property owners so I was expected to maintain the family name although my surname was not Matthews. I was constantly reminded of who I was and what was expected of me. People within the community reported our infractions and there would be consequences for our actions. My brother and uncles were seen playing marbles during class time. It was handled by my grandfather like a trial. I was called upon to testify about their behavior before they were punished.

My family had a long history with the principal. She taught my mother and her siblings so her words were considered gospel. Papa's monthly visits to the school kept me on my toes. I read and recited to the family every night after my homework was completed. My grandparents were very supportive of me and I treasured their blessings. Papa followed all the news in the Island as well as overseas; as a result I had to walk a long distance regularly to purchase the newspaper. This chore seemed to get me in the habit of reading the newspaper even as an adult. Life in the rural area was exciting, although everyone had to assist their parents on the farm, which was vital for the family's survival.

Monday was my favorite day, because my mother who was affectionately called "Lala" sent a box packed with basic necessities from Kingston for me. One of the boys would await our only public transportation which was a bus called "Magnet" to collect it. The aroma from the fish and the peppermint candy was welcomed. When there were changes in the bus schedule due to the bus breaking down on its way, the conductor would leave my box at the grocery store to be picked up. We were always delighted when Lala sent school supplies and items that were rarely sold in our area.

I roamed the countryside free-spirited, climbing trees, riding horses, accompanying my brother and uncles on their expedition of bird-shooting and fishing. I loved the tranquil hillsides, the brooks, rivers, and the endless vegetation. This was my world and I adored it. My friends met me in the place that I designated for our games as well as outdoor cooking, swimming, and horses racing. The boys in our household did the major part of the planning. This was my secret adventure; my grandparents had no knowledge of it because I provided a logical explanation for our disappearance. The boys provided the "script" for me and I just repeated what I was told to say.

One of our favorite's was catching craw-fish and making a special soup with them. There were times when I thought I ate too many different fruits, vegetables, fish, and meats, along with the regular meals. It was mandatory that I had dinner at the table so I had to find creative ways to alleviate any form of suspicion by the adults. Fresh cow's milk was served twice daily and I detested it. I made a plan that I thought would put an end to being forced to drink cows' milk. An old broken discarded fork that was being used to till the soil was close by so I used it in an effort to punch a hole in the cup, but my attempt failed. Not realizing that the force would glide off the enamel cup, I struck it really hard, one of the sharp prongs ripped through my foot. The trauma was enormous; Mama sprang into action with her antidote and stopped the excessive bleeding.

It's only God's grace that kept me alive at times because I participated in many dangerous outdoor adventures such as climbing and jumping from trees, high rocks, and into the depth of the rivers, riding untamed horses, and walking through deep bushes. These were parts of my daily routine, and it gave me a sense of freedom so I can join in singing:

I sing because I'm happy
I sing because I'm free
His eye is on the sparrow

And I know He watches me

His eye is on the sparrow And I know He watches me,

Although my mother was unhappy and protested about my daily outdoor involvement with the boys, she had very little impact because I loved this lifestyle. She attempted to put an end to it during one of her visits. She expected me to be more involved with the chores in the home. She had expected that I would demonstrate ladylike etiquette at home and in the community. Although Lala expressed her love in strange ways at times, I was more focused on my freedom. However, her rules were short-lived; I was back in business as soon as her visit ended.

My presence provided the excuses my uncles and brothers needed to avoid the consequences for not doing their chores on the farm. Papa was a disciplinarian who instilled work ethics in all of us. He constantly reminded me of the value of getting a good education and owning property, which was a top priority to him.

The thirteen and a half acres of fertile lush farmland was the pride and joy of the Matthews family. The farm was the only source of income and food source for our living. The property was fully cultivated with bananas, coconuts, chocolate, sugar cane, yams as well as numerous fruits and vegetables. The produce was sold to different companies as well as to local buyers. Domestic animals roamed freely throughout the property and they were our source of protein. Papa along with two trusted employees maintained the farm and each family member had to carry out their fair share of the responsibility.

Although we were poor, it appeared like we were among the privileged, so I considered myself a part of a middle class family. Fresh organic produce and cow's milk were taken to the kitchen daily from the farm and Mama wasted no time in preparing delicious meals for the family. Papa taught me how to read and interpret the almanac. This calendar was especially designed for farmers to know when the planting and harvesting seasons occurred.

> *To every thing there is a season, and a time to every*
> *purpose under the heaven: A time to be born, and a time*
> *to die;*
> *A time to plant, and a time to pluck up that which is*
> *planted.*
> *(Ecclesiastes 3: 1-2)*

I had numerous chores before and after school and sometimes I had the boys helping me. Listening for the crowing of roosters early in the morning was a delightful signal during the summer. Running and competing with my friends to select the best ripe mangoes under the trees were old traditions. This was a yearly event for us; children showed up from all around to fill their baskets with mangoes, followed by an afternoon feast. Rainy and hurricane seasons were challenging and also considered fun time for me. My family had to move all the animals closer to home, stock-up lots of food, cured meat, and water for the days or weeks during this season. Sometimes I could not attend school due to the heavy rain and the excessive amount of water flowing all around.

I used this time to be a teacher and few of my neighbor's children and my relatives were my students. The assignments were mainly mathematics and reading. I encouraged them to read aloud and tell their favorite stories. We sang and danced, recited and played games. *Brother Anancy Adventures* and his antics were our favorite kind of stories. I was thrilled to learn about his outrageous tricks. It inspired me to seek ways to outsmart my peers as well as my grandparents. As soon as there was a break in the showers we would run outside and play in the water. It seemed like Mama made the best meals during these rainy seasons. One of my favorite meals was the rich, hot, red pea soup, and the salt fish fritters and dumplings.

I am convinced that even at an early age, God was preparing me for great things although I could not understand it. I had a great passion for teaching and it came naturally to me. In school I would take the lead; I was outstanding in all my classes. The entire household praised me for my achievements. Looking back I can only thank God for his kindness.

> *Trust in the LORD with all thine heart;*
> *And lean not unto thine own understanding.*
> *In all thy ways acknowledge him,*
> *And he shall direct thy paths.*
> *(Proverbs 3:5-6)*

Christmas was my favorite time of the year; the aroma from the black fruitcake, the potato pudding, sorrel drink along with the endless cooking and baking created a busy atmosphere; this was a delight. Animals from our farm such as pigs, goats, and chickens were slaughtered and preserved. There were no forms of refrigeration so the creative ways to preserve the meat were to use salt and smoke. We fetched water from the river and spring that flowed through our property for all the uses in the home including drinking.

I was extremely happy that I was always assisting with mixing the sugar and butter together for the black fruitcake before Mama added the other ingredients. Baking was an all day adventure, and I loved it! I learned my cooking and baking skills from those early years in Hartland and I am grateful to Mama for sharing them with me.

All my clothes were designed and made by my grandmother. I practiced all the skills, and they were useful when I started my own family. I did the same for my daughters and they adored their homemade dresses.

One of my other duties was to run errands and take meals for some seniors who were less fortunate than we were. Mama recognized that sometimes I was reluctant to go because I wanted to have my meal first before taking theirs to them, but that was out of the question. She immediately addressed the situation although I had no clue what she was saying to me:

> *Cast your bread upon the water and thou shall find it*
> *many days after. (Ecclesiastes 11:1)*

At times, I was convinced that Mama intended to feed the entire world and I was expected to embrace this tradition after she was gone. Papa was annoyed at times because Mama constantly fed the neighbors and strangers who stopped by our home. People knew that she was always prepared and ready to comfort those who were hurting, feed the hungry, help the sick at any time of the day. We had company constantly and they were all fed, "Betty, you must always extend your kindness to the needy and God will bless you. Goodness and mercy shall follow you all the days of your life."

She would admonish me regularly, especially if she detected some signs of reluctance in me. Mama told me often that I was God's precious jewel, and I believed her. She taught me this song at an early age and we sang it together regularly:

> *Little children, little children,*
> *Who love their Redeemer,*
> *Are the jewels, precious jewels,*
> *His loved and His own.*
> *Like the stars of the morning,*
> *His bright crowns are dawning,*

They shall shine in His beauty,
Bright gems for his crown.

He will gather, He will gather
Bright gems for His kingdom;
All the pure ones, all the bright ones,
His loved and His own

I always assisted her in preparing or serving the food. I acquired my baking, cooking and sewing skills at an early age from being Mama's right hand. Grocery shopping was one of my chores and it was left up to me to be conservative with the budget.

I have often questioned myself over the years because I wanted to know God's purpose for my life. Why did Mama pick me for this job? She had nine children, why me? I came to understand what this meant as an adult as I extended kindness to others. My grandparents taught me well and in doing so they prepared me for my future. Having this strong foundation is a blessing. They have lived to see me grow and blossom into a strong successful woman. Papa was a proud man whose pride was elevated because of his granddaughter's achievements and the contributions that he had made in shaping me for my future.

As I grew, I always believed that I would excel in any subject area or anything that I wanted to do. With that in mind, I broadened my horizon at every step of the way, because my goal was to succeed at or above my fullest potential. After the experiences that Paul had in the various circumstances of life, he came to the general conclusion like me that:

I can do all things through Christ which strengtheneth
me. (Philippians 4:13)

Me, sweet sixteen.

Chapter 2
The Unexpected Move

To every thing there is a season, and a time to every
purpose under the heaven. (Ecclesiastes 3:1)

There are many pictures that flash through my mind while reflecting on my childhood. One picture that stands out the most in my memories is my family's relocation. My grandmother started visiting Kingston frequently and she was busy convincing Grandpa about something that I was determined to uncover. As I cautiously approached my grandparents' bedroom I listened keenly as they discussed some kind of financial matter. Whatever it was Papa was not a willing participant. "I must dig deeper, this seems to be something troubling to them," I thought. I was so desperate to know what their disagreement was about, so I mentioned what I observed to the boys. My brother interjected that he heard Papa talking to his best friend Mr. Palmer about how Mama hated Hartland and her desperation to move closer to her children in the city. She had never gotten accustomed to their present life-style that we thought was good in comparison to some of our friends.

Mama came from a family that was considered wealthy and she was accustomed to a better lifestyle that allowed her to have the finer things in life. Many times she complained about her disappointments. She missed the luxuries that her parents provided for her, compounded with living and working hard in Hartland to maintain her family. All four of us added what we knew; finally I came to the conclusion that there would be some changes, but what? Papa carried a burden and it was visible to us, while Mama went about as usual taking care of us. I noticed that she had restricted us from wearing some of our clothes and using a number of household items. Some of them were washed and neatly packed away. Papa was now limiting himself as well as his employees in doing their regular task on the farm. Harvesting of the crops was completed and there was no replanting of the crops in progress. Numerous questions emerged in my mind, but even then, I was still in the dark.

Late one afternoon after dinner Papa announced that we would be moving from Hartland to Kingston within a few weeks. This is the big city, the capital of Jamaica. I was stunned and confused so I blurted out unending questions. I was terrified knowing that my world was crumbling before my eyes. School was great and all my friends from birth were very close to my family. Why is this happening to me when everything is going well? I wondered what my life would be if I had to leave Hartland. The only source I had was:

Casting all your cares upon Him, for He cares for you.
(I Peter 5:7)

Tears flooded my eyes. I heard terrible stories about Kingston. Some of the stories were about children being abused. Surely, I thought if I moved I would be the next victim. The only friends I knew were here in Hartland. I was terrified, how would I cope? Based on the experiences I had during my previous visits to Kingston, I was fully aware that the culture in the city was completely different from that in the country. I was accustomed to the lifestyle in the country and I dreaded my future in the city. Children in town considered themselves to be modern, polite, and more knowledgeable of world affairs. In the meantime, a number of people felt that the culture in the city impacted some children's behavior, and they perceived it as being rude.

After much pleading and bargaining my fate was sealed. Now, I was unable to play, I felt as though I was paralyzed. I told my friends as I sought their parent's help in encouraging my grandparents to remain in Hartland. Nothing seemed to work, we were moving and I needed to be prepared for the transition. At thirteen years old I had no say in the matter, all I could do was only hope and lean on Jesus:

Leave it there, oh, leave it there
Take your burden to the Lord and leave it there
If you trust and never doubt
He would surely bring you out
Take your burden to the Lord and leave it there

I protested to no avail, all the plans for our relocation were final. I saw my world, my home, my life disappearing. There was lot of activity around the house; everything was washed and neatly packed. Mama was jubilant and Papa was serious, but working alongside her.

I sought help from my favorite teacher because she knew my family very well. She gave me some explanations about her experiences when her family had moved here and how she had protested, but it had worked out well. "Give it some time," was her encouragement. I was far from satisfied with her counseling. I informed my friends of my dilemma and how difficult it will be without them as well as life on the farm. I had lost myself in worrying and it prevented me from enjoying my daily activities. My sadness was contagious, the entire class cried when it was time to say goodbye. I felt lifeless as I slowly crawled out of my class. As I turned my head to take one last look, I decided that I would return to my school, although I didn't know how or when.

As I look back now I realize that my grandparents were seniors and were having difficulties keeping up with the farming. All of their children had grown and left Hartland for new adventures. This appeared to be the driving force for relocation as well as Mama's dislike for the country. Papa hired a truck a day before our departure; we assisted the adults for several hours in packing the items in the truck. We took a few short naps that night in anticipation of our trip.

The big day came. The Matthews family was moving to the big city--Kingston. Mama had us all dressed, then served a light breakfast early that morning. I finally crawled into the truck not wanting to talk to anyone. My eyes were clouded from my tears and I was unable to bid farewell to my friends and neighbors who stood on the sidewalk and waved at me. Mama hugged and assured me that things would be better in the city. My mother piloted Mama in finding the new property and constructed a home. Secretly, I knew my biggest fear was that I would be going to live with my parents; who would be within walking distance. I did not want that to happen. Fear had paralyzed me; my grandparents could not shield me from my apprehensions. They would have limited control. Secondly, I was angry with my mother at times for her lack of affection and support towards me. My emotions had driven me to desperation and fear. "I cannot live with them because I did not feel like I was a part of this family," I muttered. I was confronted with mixed feelings. If we were relocating farther from my parents' home it would not be so painful. God please make a way for me; but there was some comfort in this tune.

Precious Lord, take my hand
Lead me on, let me stand
I'm tired, I'm weak, I'm lone
Through the storm, through the night

Lead me on to the light Take my hand precious Lord, lead me on
When my way grows drear precious Lord linger near
When my life is almost gone
Hear my cry, hear my call
Hold my hand lest I fall
Take my hand precious Lord, lead me home

We drove for hours before stopping for lunch in a town called Bog Walk. Papa bought our favorite foods, hot patties, coco bread, and sodas. I was in no mood to eat so the boys were excited to feast on my lunch as well as theirs. There was lots of chatter about their plans, but for the first time I distanced myself from the happy group. They made several attempts to include me in the discussions, but I refused to speak. They knew that I was unhappy about the situation. Strangely, I was not angry with my grandparents although they were the ones who made their decision to relocate. In my devastation I hummed one of Mama's favorite for comfort.

No, never alone, no never alone,
He promised never to leave me,;
Never to leave me alone.

After a long four-hour ride we arrived in town. My parents waited for us at our new home. Everyone worked tirelessly to remove all of our possessions from the truck. I sat in the back of the truck hoping that I would be forgotten and taken back to Hartland. My father came and got me, he whispered, "You're going to love this place." My first night in town was difficult, my body was present, but my mind was absorbed with my future.

I had to implement a plan that would allow me to return to Hartland, but how? I will not leave my school, my friends, the flowing river and the green pastures that provided solace for me. "What can I do," I muttered. I contacted my favorite uncle seeking his help, but he did not have the solution to my problem. My second plan worked; I found every reason for them to have me boarded at my friend's house in Donnington, which was closer to my school. It was the second semester in the school year. My parents reluctantly agreed with my plan, but reminded me that I would be attending my new school after the summer break. I ended up staying for over two years. I missed my family, although I was treated well. Within a short time I became contented. My guardian was my best friend's aunt and she was a part of the household. We were the same age and we were friends from preschool so I was very happy. Both of us continued our antics together. Her family's farm was about five times the size of our farm and we roamed the bushes constantly. She had a younger brother who joined in our antics but we were less engaged in outdoor activities, such as fishing and climbing trees. Although, I was happy at their home, the rules were much different from those of Mama and Papa. This family was very generous to me and they were aware of the circumstances that existed between my mother and me. Aunt Rich and Daddy, as they were affectionately called, were prominent citizens within the community and they felt that my presence was a blessing.

My friend and I competed daily and we were ranked first or second place in class. The ranking fluctuated between us constantly, and we were proud of it. I must give my mother credit for sending my box weekly with necessities and money for my upkeep. She did this consistently and I am very grateful that she maintained me financial throughout the times that I was away from her. Although, my father's bus route on which he worked was miles away, he would travel long hours to visit me, which lasted for a short time because he had to be back on his job on time. However, I went home during the summer, and I was able to be with him and the rest of the family.

It was summer and the island was geared up for a great celebration. Crowds from every walk of life descended upon streets, alleys, churches, as well as all known public places in Kingston due to the jubilee of our Independence from Great Britain. The festive mood was contagious as the celebration engulfed every Jamaican as well as the international visitors. I was caught in a somber mood knowing that I had no friends in this crowded city. Staring in awe, I tried to comprehend the events and the expressions tempered with music, and co-mingled noise from various directions. Smiles, hugs, greetings, tears of joy made it impossible to be sad. Some seniors told stories about their ancestors, and how happy they were in their graves due to the historic event that they had witnessed. I listened intently as comparisons were made about the celebration of Emancipation Day and its impact on Independence Day. It seemed as if this would be a never-ending celebration, as food, flags, as well as other souvenirs were distributed freely. There was a sense of pride in the crowd as some shouted, "Let Freedom Ring!" There was a sense of one's own dignity, value, personal worth, self-respect, satisfaction in achievement and possession, and a proud delight that Jamaicans were ready and able to govern themselves. People took pride in the noble achievements of their ancestors and their contributions to the society.

> *O Give thanks unto the Lord; for he is good: for his mercy endureth for ever. O give thanks unto to God of gods:for his mercys endureth for ever. O give thanks to the Lord of lords: for his mercy endureth for ever. (Psalms 136: 1-3)*

The jubilation had captured people's heart and mind so they dedicated themselves to the cause. Only some of the most essential services employees had to work as most people were off from work for a weeklong celebration. Black, Gold, and Green flags decorated the entire country, while people dressed in the same symbolism. The beauty and splendor took over the streets, business establishments, and the homes of the people. I was away from my home school; my parents wanted me to be a part of the celebration so I went along with my brothers to Greenwich All Age School in Kingston.

My first visit to the school in Kinston was August 6, 1962, the day of our first Independence celebration. I had every reason to avoid the city school where my siblings attended because the students made fun of me; I did not fit in. Some referred to me as "country girl" while others stared and laughed while pointing at me. I was miserable due to the ongoing teasing; I wanted to cry or just keep running away to avoid them. Jamaica, the land of wood and water had gained its independence from Great Britain after decades of Colonial Rule. After repeating our new Pledge of Allegiance, the music bellowed our first National Anthem:

> *Eternal Father bless our land*
> *Guard us with Thy mighty hand.*
> *Keep us free from evil powers*
> *Be our light through countless hours*
> *To our leaders, Great Defender,*
> *Grant true wisdom from above*
> *Justice, truth, be ours forever,*
> *Jamaica Land we Love.*
> *Jamaica, Jamaica, Jamaica*
> *Land we love.*

I tried to make sense of what was in progress. It was evident that

23

the children were all prepared for the celebration; I was not. Their music teachers had fine-tuned the entire program and the students were proud of their renditions. I was very conscious of my green and gold uniform that had a lighter shade than the other students—allowing me to be spotted easily. I wanted to rip it off of my body. I was enraged inside as I wondered why my mother made me wear this ugly outfit. If only my uniform were like the other students then I would blend in. After the assembly the principal announced, "Students please go to your classes." At that moment I was baffled and confused not having a class to call my own. Although, my younger brother was in the fourth grade I followed him to his class. He was the only person that I knew. What a disaster! The teacher interrogated me about my presence there while the students giggled. Maybe if my mother had sought permission from the school then I would not be put in this embarrassing position. I really felt like an intruder, eyes pierced me throughout this ordeal. The children all had their friends and I was the loner. Finally, the teacher allowed me to remain in her class.

Every child was given a gift, but my gift was inferior to her students. My brother was with his friends and he took quick glances at me. I suspected that he was embarrassed because he feared the worst. "George, is this your sister? Why is she here? She should be at her school," remarked the teacher to him. My brother was dumbfounded; he gave no reply. The teacher seemed annoyed but walked away from him. "God, why am I here," I muttered. This was one of the worst days in my life. I was as friendly as possible but no one seemed to care or wanted to be the friend of a country girl. As I watched with amazement this song became alive in my heart:

> *Be not dismayed whate'er betide,*
> *God will take care of you;*
> *Beneath His wings of love abide,*
> *God will take care of you.*
>
> *God will take care of you,*
> *Through every day, o'er all the way;*
> *He will take care of you,*
> *God will take care of you.*

I craved one of the adorable cups with the Coat of Arms, instead I got a small green metal cup that meant very little to me. I wanted to experience the full excitement and happiness of Independence, but it was dashed by the circumstances. This magnitude of celebration could never be recaptured for the rest of my life although Jamaicans celebrate their Independence yearly in a grand style. The outpouring of expressions, feelings of gratitude, love, pain, hardship, achievement, the re-establishment of a new parliament, was a breath of fresh air and a new direction for the country. The empowerment of each individual was evident. Jamaicans are known for their strong sense of self-identity expressed through music, food, and rich cultural mix that extends far beyond its shores.

My mind raced back to Donnington Elementary School where provisions were made for me and I imagined my friends were having a great time. My emotions got the better of me and it was difficult to extract the tears. The feelings of isolation and rejection while you are a child can be interpreted as a cruel form of abandonment and punishment. My imagination took over and it created a sense of celebration in my old school.

After awhile it appeared like I was just dreaming--this is not real. This was my only way of coping with the fear as well as the rejection. My first Independence was a total disaster that will remain with me for life. I had to muster all the strength in me to sit through this torture. No one extended any form of empathy so I was the first one to bolt through the door and run home at the end of the school celebration. The others stayed behind with their friends and enjoyed the music and food along with other fun activities.

Although I am the second child among my eleven siblings, the feeling of being lost was overwhelming. We loved one another, but I just felt like a misfit in the group. I came from an environment where I was considered the "little princess" and now I had to be contented with a much lower position, if any at all. I was convinced that my younger brother was the "king" in this household. It seemed like I had no intention of adjusting to my situation and this negative experience had strengthened my case. I knew no matter what had happen I would succeed so my strength came from these words:

> *And he shall be like a tree planted by the rivers of water,*
> *That bringeth forth his fruit in his season;*
> *His leaf also shall not wither;*
> *And whatsoever he doeth shall prosper. (Psalms 1:3)*

Sunday evenings were our favorite because we were given the opportunity to take a walk in our neighborhood and get an ice-cream cone. On our return we all ate a slice of potato or cornmeal pudding before bed, which was prepared by my mother. As a child I anticipated this treat with glee. At some point I started to stand by the window of a church and watched the services. I paid special attention to the testimonies; a lot of the church participants were in my age group. The Minister invited me to the service, but my Mom was not thrilled with their form of worship. She did not favor the Pentecostal Church because she did not understand the manifestation of the Holy Spirit. I continued my visits, which enraged my mother so I lost my privileges. Whenever my father was home he would say, "Let her go."' So I was happy. One night during testimony service I was moved, convicted by the Holy Spirit as we sang:

> *Once like a bird in prison I dwelt,*
> *No freedom from my sorrow I felt*
> *But Jesus came and listened to me,*
> *Glory to God, He set me free!*
>
> *He set me free, yes, He set me free,*
> *He broke the bonds of prison for me*
> *I'm glory bound my Jesus to see,*
> *Glory to God, He set me free!*

There I gave my heart to God. This was a new beginning in my life; I felt an unimaginable peace within me. I immersed myself in my bible and singing of hymns.

> *When the Savior reached down for me*
> *When he reached down His hand for me*
> *I was lost and undone, without God or His Son*
> *When he reached down His hand for me*
>
> *I was near to despair when He came to me there*
> *And He showed me that I could be free*
> *Then He lifted my feet, gave me gladness complete*
> *When He reached down His hand for me*

I was rejoicing as I came home singing. That night I sat all night outside as the consequence for going to church and staying until the end of the service. Several leaders from the church visited my home to discuss and explain my new direction, but this did not resolve the matter. My mother was annoyed with my blatant disregard for her rules and forbid me from going to that church anymore.

My mother saw that I was determined to attend services so my freedom was curtailed even more. I was convicted, saved, filled with the Holy Ghost and there was no way I would stop praising God. I recruited as many adults as I could to speak on my behalf, but she was resolute. I had a burning desire to worship God. There were numerous consequences but I endured them all. She verbalized her disappointment, but honestly she did not understand that God had called me and He was preparing me for service. "Velma your major dreams should be your education, not church." Although, I was denied some opportunities this did not stop me from achieving my goals because God made it possible for me to succeed. He has blessed me consistently throughout the years. I concurred with the Apostle Paul when he expressed himself clearly that we have access to God's blessings through prayer.

> *Now unto him that is able to do exceeding, abundantly,*
> *above all that we ask or think, according to the power*
> *that worketh in us. (Ephesians 3:20)*

It was in April, just days before my seventeenth birthday when I took my vows, "I will serve you Jesus until death." My grandmother discovered my baptism due to my wet clothes so I begged her, "Don't share my secret." My baptism could not remain a secret and this really angered my mom because she did not give her permission for me to be baptized. Secondly, she was against this entire concept of me taking up my time with this church. I stood up for what I believed then and now.

> *I will never leave you nor forsake you. (Hebrews 13:5)*

Although my conviction led to limited opportunities, I had confidence in my Savior and I had no intention of backing down. I felt the hand of God's protection and it had strengthened me during an unpleasant encounter. I was so happy as I imparted what I had learned and was experiencing as a young Christian.

There was a young male acquaintance that stopped by the church at times and I began to impart the word of God to him. Shortly after, I was on my way to see my friend in the same complex when he offered to show me his apartment. I agreed and walk over to see it. While I was standing in the living room, he pointed out some improvements that had been done recently. Without warning he locked the door. I quickly realized that I was in danger of being raped. I commanded him to open the door, but he suddenly acted as if he were deaf. As he attempted to hold me down on his couch, I looked him in his face and shouted three times, "The blood of Jesus, touch not the Lord's anointed!!" I felt a power of the Holy Spirit over me, and I began to speak in unknown tongues as the Spirit gave me utterance. Fear took hold of him, he appeared that some shock waves had taken hold of him; he quickly opened the door and I left the apartment full of God's anointing. I walked out praising God for His deliverance. This was the first major test of my conviction, and right there I realized that I serve a very powerful God. I refused to yield to the enemy because Jesus had equipped me with power from on high.

> *Yield not to temptation, for yielding is sin;*
> *Each vict'ry will help you some other to win;*
> *Fight manfully onward, dark passions subdue;*
> *Look ever to Jesus, He'll carry you through.*

> *Ask the Savior to help you,*
> *Comfort, strengthen, and keep you;*
> *He is willing to aid you,*
> *He will carry you through.*

I did not understand where God was leading me but I knew He was with me. It was not long before I was mentoring the youth in my church and in the community. I served as a 4H club leader and through my work others were led to the Lord. Throughout my life, I have always been determined to achieve my goal. As I grew and became older I realized that with God all things are possible and He has called me for a purpose.

Chapter 3
An Unexpected Encounter

$\bowtie$

*All things work together for the good of those that love the Lord
and are called according to his purpose. (Romans 8:28)*

Living with my parents meant following the family rules and to be in
Sunday school on time every week. Wherever I was, if I heard the chime
from "Back to the Bible" I knew I had to hurry home, get dressed as fast as
I could and be in Sunday school on time. In Sunday school, I was rewarded
if I could recite my Bible verse. It was a pleasure because my reward was
always a beautiful card with a new scripture verse. At the end of the year,
the cards were tallied and the winners were rewarded with special gifts
for Christmas. I boasted about my collection of cards as well my ability
to recite my scripture verses correctly. Some of my siblings, who I had a
healthy competition with, had difficulties in studying and reciting their
verse of scripture, so I acquired more cards as well as gifts than they did.

During one of my visits to church a young man approached me and
asked if I would be willing to give him one of my treasured Sunday school
cards. I pondered, "Why would he need this card? He doesn't attend our
Sunday school." Still I obliged. He and his family were noted to be quiet
but faithful members of the church. I dispelled the thought of his actions
but I had no regrets, knowing that I had one card less would not impede
me from receiving my prize. This unusual encounter lacked every element
of the norm; the request came out of nowhere. My acquaintance with
Matthew came about through a scripture card; the scripture verse that was
written in bold print read:

> *Were not ten cleansed but where are the nine. (Luke
> 17:17)*

It was impossible not to observe this young man because he was
helpful to the congregation. At the time, it did not appear that he had
any interest in me. My friends and I did not pay him any attention; we
did not consider him to be in our league because he was an introvert. My

friends and I were more attuned to social activities. I was more engaged in educational matters. I was determined to have a college degree. On the contrary he showed very little interest in social life while his focus was on church activities and his job as a carpenter. Who would ever think that he was paying attention to *my* daily activities?

About a year later, Grant, one of Matthew's friends invited all of us to his wedding in rural St. Thomas. I had completely forgotten the incident with the card not knowing that it would resurface. St. Thomas' hills were very difficult to climb but the scenery was breathtaking; I lagged a long way behind the entire party as we walked from the church to the reception at Grant's home. Matthew waited for me seeing that I was walking alone. As I came close he muttered, "When it is our time to get married I will not take you this far." This took me by surprise. My strength was renewed and I raced to find my best friend and shared his comments. We laughed out of control and I thought, "Maybe he is crazy. I certainly would not want him to be my husband." I became exhausted from the long travel as well as walking up the steep hill so I was offered a room to rest during the reception. Although people bustled in and out of the room I fell asleep within minutes of lying on the bed. I opened my eyes just in time to see Matthew standing close to the door staring at me with his hands full of ripe mangoes that he had collected outside, "I saved these for you." I did not respond; I got up quickly and join the festivity. I was puzzled as I wondered, how long was he standing there watching me and who appointed him to be my guard. As a result of his comment while walking up the hill, I constantly avoided him.

Weeks later Matthew became very ill, the youth group was asked to visit him during his illness, but I deliberately stayed home. I refused to go to his home for that may give him some false notion. At that time I was employed by the church in their early childhood program. After his recovery he showed up at the school, but I pretended that I did not see him. Later that afternoon, we ran into each other on the street; he stopped, trying to involve me in a conversation, but I kept walking. Suddenly my attention was drawn to the card that he pulled out of his pocket as if he wanted me to look at it. "Do you remember this?"

"What do you want?" I enquired making it a point to be rude.

He replied in a calm manner, "I kept praying for a wife and the Lord showed me this card, *Were not ten cleansed but where are the nine,* in a strange vision and said that you are my wife."

"What did you say? Wife, Wife! Not interested!" I stated my rejection in an angry tone, while staring at him in a scornful manner hoping he would disappear. Although he was rebuffed, he was now more convinced than ever that this was God's plan for his life; unbeknown to me he pursued me in his humble way.

I was eighteen and thinking about continuing my studies. Anger had set in as well as confusion due to his persistence. I dreamt that night that he brought me a gift and it was one of the most beautiful gold rings that I have ever seen. One of my friends took it and he insisted that it was mine. I woke up feeling afraid so I visited Yvonne my friend and poured out my anger to her. She said "Velma, that's a decent family, they are poor but caring and I think you should consider it." WHAT!!!!!!!!!!!!.

To add to my frustration Matthew showed up at my parent's home unannounced. As I responded to the knock on the gate I saw him. You dare not come here, who invited you? I was shaking but he was resolute. Panic struck me when I saw him, "Matthew, why are you here? Have you lost your mind? I don't know who wants you." Tears flooded my eyes as I ran and hid behind the house. My Dad invited him inside thinking that he stopped by from the church just to say hello, not knowing who he was. Time evaporated, it could have been ten or fifteen minutes during the visit my father called me to sit with them. Papa kept calling me until I appeared. "Betty, Betty, I need you right now! A young man is here to see you." I held back as long as I could but I had to obey. Within minutes of my appearance my father announced that this young man is here to ask me for your hand in marriage. Do you know him? I felt like a rock was stuck in my throat.

I had a good rapport with my father, but I was lost for words, and I felt a great deal of embarrassment. I could not convince my father or anyone that I was not aware of this situation, so I hung my head in silence and shame. My dad sought some explanation as well as answers from me because he was willing to abide by my wishes. He was unaware that I was not involved with Matthew, he was almost a stranger. My dad and I were both taken by surprise and I was consumed with so much anger that I could not defend myself. "At no time did I invite this man to my home; I don't want to have anything to do with him," I whispered to myself. My mom was apprehensive; she listened and observed, but did not show too much interest in his request while my father was very polite. "Young man, if my daughter agrees to marry you, then I will give you her hand in marriage." He gave his lecture and his expectations, then he said "These are my rules, both of you must not be seen hanging around on the streets talking or fooling around, everything must be done decently and in order."

Matthew left my home rather pleased after meeting my parents. This gave him the start that he wanted, so he continued his pursuit. I was not able to function due to the shock that I experienced that Sunday evening. I was desperate to talk to my best friend Yvonne concerning this intrusion; I was devastated. I totally lost my sense of direction.

My parents were now convinced that I had a lover, I thought. I was helpless. I considered this the darkest day of my life; I was determined to get even with this man that I had never dated. I did not have an inch of affection or interest in him. I was extremely bitter about what had happened to me because I just did not understand it. I felt weak and useless but I took comfort in God's words:

> *And he said unto me, My grace is sufficient for thee: for my strength is made perfect in weakness. (2 Corinthians 12:9)*

After this incident I wanted to get away from my parents house because this strange encounter had just compounded my problems. It was not long before I started living with my grandparents again. I sought refuge in their home and I knew at no time would they turn me away. The love and bond that we shared was unbreakable, they were willing to make sacrifices for my well being. Secondly, there were no restrictions for me to attend church worship services and that was the desire of my heart. Whenever Matthew tried to visit me, I pretended that I was not at home, and I had a relative to support my claim. He would find a way to hang around hoping that I would appear.

The months that followed were challenging. After a few months of my grand schemes, I finally was caught off guard. I was home alone one Sunday evening and I answered the door and there he was. This was during the time that Matthew would be normally teaching Sunday school at church, so this was unexpected. I was too frightened to react, and there was nowhere for me to hide. I tried to act calm hoping a family member would arrive home. I wasted no time in informing him that my grandmother was away but she would be home soon. He asked if he could come in sit and wait for her arrival. I could not talk my way out so he informed me that he would wait for her. Slowly he walked in and sat down without waiting for my response. Within a short time he demanded an answer from me as to when I would be his bride. I was desperate for him to leave; suddenly I muttered, "August." He enquired, "August when and what time?" Trembling, I whispered, "10th, 20th or 24th." At this point I was willing to provide any false information that would signal his departure. "Four, five o'clock," I blurted out. He realized how nervous I was and used it to his advantage after all these months of rejection. Although my heart was racing I did not feel like I was in danger. I was not terrified of him but the prospect of his views regarding marriage, as well as the possibility of my major dream of going to college to become a teacher could be at odds with his. I was just a young Christian who was learning to keep the faith. I was just beginning to learn about trials and temptations that some early Christians endured, but I did not perceive my situation as trials, instead I saw it as a man fighting to own me. At no time during this ordeal was I able to make any connection to Paul's testimony, which is true:

> *My brethren, count it all joy when ye fall into divers temptations; Knowing this, that the trying of your faith worketh patience. (James 1:2-3)*

As I reflected on previous events, I was certain that I did not give this young man any reason to think that I wanted to be his friend, becoming his wife would be even a more far- fetched idea. Once a week I attended the youth meeting; a number of us would walk home and the brothers would make sure the girls got home safely. He accompanied us although he had his bicycle that he normally rides home. I was the first one to reach home but he asked if he could speak to me while the others accompanied the other girls. I obliged, "What is he up to now?" He calmly presented me with one of the most beautiful engagement rings, "This is for you. I hope you'll like it." I was enraged by this gesture so I grabbed the ring and tossed it in the street and it fell into a dirty gutter. I wished it would be lost forever. I stormed off to my home leaving him searching for it while refusing to look back. "What will it take for this man to understand?" I crawled into bed not knowing what to do or how to get rid of him. I laid in bed that night examining all my options that were available to me in an attempt to escape. The possibility of relocating was eminent, and that would be the solution to this problem.

Three years prior to this incident, one of my favorite aunts and her husband wanted me to join them in London. They would be my guardians while I attended college. Some of the required documents were not submitted with the application to the British Consulate and as a result the papers lingered for a long time without being processed. Final efforts were made at the last minute to complete the process. It was mandatory that a copy of my birth certificate be sent in within the allotted time. However, it arrived too late to meet the deadline of the age restriction for minors. As there were no valid reasons for the delay, my British visa was denied. I was absolutely sure that my departure would put an end to this madness. It was extremely disappointing when my aunt sent the letter of denial from the British Consulate to my mother. Only God knows why my birth certificate was withheld, and I lost my chance to travel to London. I felt like all hope had failed. What's next! I continued to believe the word of God even in my worst situation:

> *You have made known to me the ways of life; you shall make me full of joy with your countenance. (Acts 2:1)*

Matthew appeared at my door a number of times and I managed to escape by asking my cousin to make excuses on my behalf that she handled poorly due to her young age. He caught my grandmother's attention and she was drawn to his good manners and soon he became her favorite so he had no trouble showing up at our home. Both of them would engage in long, lively discussions. This was not good I thought because he had an excuse to be at my home and I certainly didn't want him coming here. We made short exchanges when I had to come in the living room and I made no inquiry about the incident pertaining to the ring he bought me. I strictly avoided any form of conversation hoping that would deter him. I maintained a distance between us while my grandmother adored their discussions. I realized that she was unaware of my disgust toward this young man and that made matters worse. Several times she made comments about her conservation with him and tried to seek my opinion, but I quickly changed the subject. My behavior was now noticeable to her so she said, "Betty don't you think this is one of the finest young man in Kingston?"

"Mama have you forgotten that you left the dinner on the stove cooking? I can smell something burning." She jumped to her feet, hoping to save our dinner as well as our home from a fire. Due to my announcement her attention shifted to a more important matter. I knew my response was unimportant at this juncture so I eluded her question. She returned grateful that we were not in any danger of a fire.

I had to share my innermost thoughts with someone; I confided in my best friend's aunt, Mrs. Rich. She was my guardian whom I boarded with when my family moved from Hartland. I traveled from Kingston to her home one afternoon--she was excited to see me. My best friend and her brother were no longer living with her; they had migrated to their parents in England. After I rested from my long trip, I informed her of my mission. My heart was burdened with this matter so I poured my heart out to her. I spent a week relating my sorrows only to find that she had viewed it as a blessing. She did not support my views, however, she remained neutral; she was desperate just to meet him before giving her verdict. Her advice was general but it left me agreeing to be more civil towards him during this time. I thanked her, and then boarded the bus, sat motionless as the bus sped away. I kept singing and hoping that this problem would disappear.

Why Should I Feel Discouraged

Why should I feel discouraged,
Why should the shadows come,
Why should my heart be lonely
And long for heav'n and home,
When Jesus is my portion?
My constant Friend is he:

His eye is on the sparrow,
And I know he watches me;
His eye is on the sparrow,
And I know he watches me.

"Let not your heart be troubled,"
His tender Word I hear,
And resting on his goodness,
I lose my doubt and fear;
Though by the path he leadeth
But one step I may see:

Whenever I am tempted,
Whenever clouds arise,
When songs give place to sighing,
When hope within me dies,
I draw the closer to him,
From care he sets me free;

Weeks later, she finally met him and her impression of him seemed positive. I was not convinced. I thought that I was just too young to get married. I was not fortunate in getting any support; everyone seems to like him except me. She stated that she had detected some outstanding qualities in him and she was proud of the step that he was taking as a young man. She continued by saying he would make a fine husband. She had no idea of the wound that she had pierced through my heart. "How did she arrive at that conclusion when she barely knew him?" I mumbled. I had no one supportive of my concerns all they could think of is what a decent, honest, and hard-working Christian he was. I have always thought that Ms. Rich was a good judge of character, but not this time. I had to take courage as I moved forward:

> *Courage, sister, do not stumble,*
> *Though thy path be dark as night;*
> *There's a star to guide the humble:*
> *Trust in God and do the right.*
> *Let the road be rough and dreary,*
> *And its end far out of sight,*
> *Foot it bravely; strong or weary,*
>
> *Trust in God, trust in God,*
> *Trust in God and do the right.*
>
> *Perish policy and cunning,*
> *Perish all that fears the light!*
> *Whether losing, whether winning,*
> *Trust in God, and do the right.*

I tried hard to keep calm but elusive. Early one Saturday morning Matthew stopped by and he brought some special selected fruits and vegetables for my grandmother. I knew it was intended for me but I accepted it gracefully for her and thanked him. My eyes bulged seeing the size and quality of the fruits and vegetables that he dropped off. While turning to leave he said "May I ask you a simple favor?" Oh God what now, I said to myself.

"Please, please would you be kind enough to allow me to take....you to Hope Botanical Gardens... I just need a little time to explain myself."

This garden was a popular tourist attraction and it was one of the most beautiful well-kept gardens in the country. "I would appreciate it a lot," he appealed. He seemed so sorrowful that I unwillingly agreed.

He arrived at my home early the following Saturday, he waited on me patiently. We rode the city bus to Hope Gardens. As soon as we arrived we roamed the garden talking and observing the different species of flowers as we walked carefully through the maze while trying not to get lost. He was very careful in his mannerism hoping that this is the break that he was awaiting. This was the first time that we had a pleasant discussion and we partially enjoyed each other's company. After about two hours the subject of the wedding emerged so I sat on the grass and listened quietly. He encouraged me not to be afraid because he would be a good husband, father, brother, and a true friend to me. I was caught off guard when I was landed our first kiss and it was a total disaster so we pretended that it had never happened and I cried. I did not rebel for too long, because he apologized for his insensitivity. It took some time before he was able to repair the damage but we returned to our conversation. We spent the entire day talking while enjoying the beautiful scenery of this great place. We even had lunch there, although I was too timid to enjoy the food. Somehow we started to discuss the wedding and some tentative plans. He suggested that his mom, a professional seamstress, would be delighted to design and sew my wedding dress. There was a little breakthrough and he accompanied me back home before dark. The situation was still tense but some progress was made. Spending an entire day together in a garden was a great way to begin our relationship.

> *Be careful for nothing; but in every thing by prayer and supplication with thanksgiving let your requests be made known unto God. (Philippians 4:6)*

What a mess I had gotten myself into. He had no doubts that he had been successful in his quest. As the saga dragged on, I realized that I had to free myself from the false promises I had made. He was extremely delighted, so he went ahead and informed our minister of his plans for marriage without my knowledge. I was summoned to my minister's office. Too afraid to protest, I sat like a lamb to the slaughter and listened. Based on church rules, prospective couples were given three months after an announcement is made to have their marriage done. The clock began ticking after our second meeting; he was to be relieved of all his church duties pending his marriage. The minister saw my reluctance and enquired about my goals and intentions. I informed him of my plans for college. He was in favor of it and he also hinted that I could find a better suitor as well. The minister was puzzled because this was not the norm for young couples.

They were generally excited and sometimes in a hurry to go to the altar. He studied me carefully, because he knew there was something missing. He stared into my blank face as he gave his fatherly speech concerning how we are expected to conduct ourselves as unto the Lord. My thoughts were miles away and not focused on a word that my spiritual leader was saying. All I wanted at that moment was for this man to drop his crazy plan.

Although, I maintained a good relationship with the church members, only my friend Yvonne was aware of my feelings. Minister T couldn't get any information from me so he dismissed us with the understanding that we should return soon. The look that I gave Matthew could tell the whole story; I detested him because I was ambushed the second time. I felt like I was pressed out of measure by this man who was nine years older than I.

> *Even the youths shall faint and be weary, and the young men shall utterly fall: But they that wait upon the Lord shall renew their strength; they shall mount up with wings as eagles; they shall run, and not be weary; and they shall walk, and not faint. (Isaiah 40:30-31)*

One of my friends made it clear that Matthew was the most generous and decent person that she had met; she was confident that we would be a good match. It appeared that love was not being considered as a first step towards marriage. Now that I had half-heartedly agreed to his proposal the time was drawing close and I realized that I had to do or die. One of my greatest supporters was Mrs. Rich, she was the aunt of my best friend from kindergarten, and she took the lead role. My grandmother and my dad were supportive while my mother was apprehensive and kept her distance. Matthew's mother and his siblings supported him and embraced me at first sight. His mom was ecstatic as she creatively designed my silver and white bridal dress, which was one of her most stunning designs. Mrs. Rich put in motion the entire cake designs, as a professional in this area. She prepared a nine layer cake for my wedding reception in Kingston and a six layer cake for the reception in Donnington at her bungalow home. Mrs. Rich had no children and she was very proud of me. She was determined to have a repeat of the wedding in the area in which I had attended school, hoping that my school friends would have a chance to attend my wedding. This was the rural area where I attended school and many of my friends and family still resided there. The two weddings were planned ten days apart. While the wedding preparation was in full gear the expected bride was in a state of panic.

Marriage on the Horizon

There is no fear in love; but perfect love casteth out fear: because fear hath torment. He that feareth is not made perfect in love. (John 4:18)

Matthew and I corresponded a little better but not enough to warrant a wedding. Friends and family were ecstatic and this seemed to be thrilling and exciting in some ways. Matthew's fears grew because he was not sure if I would disappear at the eleventh hour and leave him standing at the altar. I appeared dull and distant and that was killing him. Finally, the big day came; I refused to talk with Matthew two days before the wedding. He could not resist the urge to direct his driver to stop by my house while he was on his way to church. This was unheard of because this is considered a bad omen in our culture. The groom should not see his bride on the wedding day before the wedding ceremony. His appearance startled me; he said that he needed to be sure that I would be coming. He was afraid that he would be left at the altar not knowing what to do. He observed the tears flowing down my face and very little was done in the way of getting dressed for my wedding. "Please get dressed and be at the church he beseeched; I will take care of you. I promise to be the best husband. I will be waiting at the church for you." The words seem to stick in my ears. What am I doing with myself? Love was not evident to me even at this point; maybe I did not know what love was.

As he walked out, I could see that he was contemplating his fate. His best man did what he could to stop him from coming to my home but he was unsuccessful. Grandma intervened, "Betty it's time, let's get dressed, don't let him wait too long for your hand." My two friends who were given the task of getting me ready were as confused as I. They did their best to move things along but I was in no hurry to get dressed. The event appeared to me more like a punishment instead of a celebration. I was emotionally drained and confused, I wanted an escape route. My thoughts strayed to my family and the damaging effect this would have created for them as well. Finally, I relented and I was fully prepared for my wedding, then I set off to the church. My silver and white apparel stood out but I was not in the mood for the occasion. As the musician played the bridal procession, I felt like I was in a dream.

As I strolled down the aisle of the church I kept my face strait not making eye contact with anyone--not even the groom. My bridal party was all in place unaware that I was an unwilling bride. I was led to the altar as a sheep ready to be slaughtered on August 28, 1968. My maid of honor's job that day had increased; she had to keep my face dry throughout the event. As the wedding ceremony began, my eyes were lowered to the floor. I can't even recall most of the ceremony. I was hoisted on an emotional roller coaster. The entire ceremony appeared to last for ages as I mumbled the words of my vows. Matthew kept touching me, alerting me to smile. What a relief when the ceremony ended. I walked out quickly passing my guests without even stopping to greet them or to even admire the colorful and joyful scenery. I spent very little time around the area before I requested that we leave the church in a hurry. We rode around while I tried to compose myself before taking the pictures and attending the wedding reception. It was a very difficult task, but I had to get a grip on my emotions.

> *And the Lord shall guide thee continually, and satisfy*
> *thy soul in drought, and make fat thy bones; and thou*
> *shall be like a watered garden, and like a spring of water,*
> *whose waters fail not. (Isaiah 58:11)*

"Everything is going to be fine V; this is what God wants for us." My husband established my new name at that point "V". He took me to a private garden away from everyone so that I could gain control of myself. Here he did his best to console me. When we entered the wedding reception, I was drained but I tried to make the best of everything. As the festivity grew I began to greet my guests. It was exciting; everyone drank and ate to their heart's content. I was extremely careful as well as tactful in my movements fearing I would revert to my old condition. I had surprised myself after this drawn out ordeal that I finally became a married woman at the age of 19. Before the reception ended I felt some life but I was too weak to enjoy the splendid meal that was being prepared for us. My husband found himself being my chaperone due to how frail I was emotionally. His family adores him, and they also took a leading role in the wedding. They were unaware of the circumstances that existed between us.

We arrived home late that night exhausted after the wedding. What will happen now that he is my husband? I dreaded that night; I was extremely tense but he remained calm. Slowly, I removed my garments. "Don't look this way." The first night ended without romance. "I will wait until you are ready," he muttered. So we went to bed.

His love and patience were present at all times. He consistently showered me with kindness. Sometimes I would be awaken by his movements and it was to get something prepared for me or just making sure no mosquitoes are anywhere near to me. He would prepare my breakfast before leaving for work. He did most of the chores in the house even if I protested, "I will wash the dishes." Sometimes I questioned myself, "Why did I despise this man so much but finally go along with his proposal?" After months of uncertainty love started to emerge but the process was slow. We were now a couple but he was willing to wait on my love as well as romance. I was in no haste for romance and I cried frequently thinking that I had made a big mistake. I knew what to expect but the timing and person was not what I wanted. He was extremely gentle as he assured me that with God everything is going to work out fine. Whatever I needed he would be ready to get it as long as it was in his powers. I was fearful that my dreams would be lost but on the contrary he was supportive and encouraged me to reach for the stars. He also reminded me of his favorite scripture:

Love is patient and kind. Love is not jealous or boastful or proud. (1Corinthians 13:4)

Matthew's kindness, love, and patience and understanding were unbelievable; he treated me like a queen. I was mesmerized by his qualities and sometimes I tested his patience but he remained the same. I enjoyed listening to his harmonious voice of praises and worship as well as moments that he serenaded me. It is impossible to say when we found true love but when I did it meant every letter in the word- LOVE. Matthew was always protective of me even when we walked on the streets. I am not sure what this really meant, all I knew is that I was and still am treated as a queen. After eight months of marriage and we were much closer he practically pleaded with me for us to move out of my grandparents home and establish our own home. I was not ready to venture on my own. "V", as he affectionately calls me, "It is time for us to be on our own." I was still reluctant to relocate so he gave me a speech about the responsibility of a husband. He reminded me that the scripture states that he must be a provider, a priest, and a protector. I saw his determination, so I cooperated and we finally moved in to our new apartment. We did not have all the necessities that were needed but we were happy. Our lives revolved around the Church and the teaching of the Bible; and he was fully committed to the Lord. Although he worked very hard, he was delighted to carry out chores in the house even if he was tired.

During the years our relationship has blossomed and I now believe that it was all meant to be. We joke about our past sometimes; I would tease him by saying that he stole me from my grandparents home, and he would respond by saying, you had no business to follow a stranger. Based on the experiences that I had, my confidence has been strengthen by Christ's words to Paul:

> *And he said unto me, My grace is sufficient for you: for my strength is made perfect in weakness. Most gladly therefore will I rather boast in my weaknesses, that the power of Christ may rest upon me. (2 Corinthians 12:9)*

Matthew and I started to build a very strong relationship in our marriage; I have never experience so much love, peace and happiness in my life and it made me feel contented. We both traveled to work in different places so we rode the city bus. While on my way to work in Kingston a package that I was carrying fell on the floor in the bus, in my attempt to retrieve the package my wedding bands flew off my finger. Some of the passengers on the bus assisted in the search but I did not recover my wedding bands. The loss of my wedding band made me distraught. I arrived home sad and very disgruntled. Matthew noticed the change and felt a bit uneasy. Within minutes he enquired about my day at work and my trip back home. I was reluctant to talk. Finally I gained the courage to inform Matthew about the loss and the circumstances that led to it. His response was shocking, "Whatever don't cost life don't cost anything. I will replace it." He offered to replace my ring several times, but I kept refusing. I was really hurt and I don't think the new ring would have the same significance to me. After years of rejecting his offer, he finally replaced it on his own without my input. This time one of my rings had a beautiful diamond and I accepted it with pleasure. After years of living together, I came to understand the prayer of David and how similar it is to my life.

> *The Lord is my shepherd; I shall not want.*
> *He maketh me to lie down in green pastures:*
> *He leadeth me beside the still waters.*
> *He restoreth my soul:*
> *He leadeth me in the paths of righteousness for his name's sake.*
> *Yea, though I walk through the valley of the*
> *shadow of death; I will fear no evil: for thou*

art with me; thy rod and thy staff they
comfort me.
Thou preparest a table before me in the
presence of mine enemies: thou anointest
my head with oil; my cup runneth over.
Surely goodness and mercy shall follow me all
the days of my life; and I will dwell in the
house of the Lord forever.

Our wedding, August 1968.

An African festivity, June 2008.

Chapter 4
God's Gifts

Be fruitful and multiply. (Genesis 1:28)

Although my wedding was a few months old it was a blur; I was unable to remember what was said at the ceremony or at the reception. As I struggled to make sense of this matter, I suddenly became embarrassed because my wedding day should have been the most important day of my life, serving as a life-long memory. It took some time for the entire matrimonial service and its significance to register in my mind and when it did, I began a new chapter in my life.

Our relationship had began to blossom to the point that there were no reasons to doubt that we had become one in body base on the vows. I developed a sense of security as he maintained his job as a mason/carpenter while I worked and attend college. Although I was building my life as a young Christian in the church, I was involved with numerous activities and this became the center of our lives. I became a Sunday school teacher, youth director, and a leader and mentor in a 4H Club. Working with the youth and their parents was a delight because we had a lot in common and I was able to relate to their experiences. Many of them sought counseling in spiritual, social, personal, and educational issues.

In our first year I was very happy as we maintained a simple lifestyle. However, there was one problem that bothered me. Matthew did not share in a lot of discussions or dialogue; this weighed heavily on me at times. "Please say something," I often implored. "I would like to know your thoughts and feeling about the actions that we have taken on different situations." I gathered the feeling that if I loved something that is all that matters to him and I detested that kind of behavior. I noticed that he had more interest in studying my character as well as my manner more than sharing his thoughts. One thing that he treasured most was that we worshipped God together. His actions as well as his commitment gave a new meaning to be a faithful husband, as well as one who help to strengthening my faith. He became my best friend; he was never judgmental and I was never fearful of sharing my innermost thoughts and my past experiences.

Money was limited so we purchased only the things that were needed for our home, and very little remained for social events.

I questioned myself at times as to what the Lord was preparing me for. I was aware that it was a special task although I was not able to define it. I had an urge that allows me to serve people in several different ways. One of His gifts that I have recognized over the years is that I am able to work with people through the worst storms of their lives and bring hope as they received their victories. What makes this so special is that in most cases they wandered in my path. Most of them did not know me, but they felt comfortable to open up to me. Some of these situations were complex, and difficult, but I was happy to consult Christ for direction.

After three years of marriage, I recognized that Matthew was becoming really desperate to have children. After a long discussion we decided to seek medical attention. We were tested medically and it was determined from the results that he was fine. My results however, revealed some gynecological problems that could hinder pregnancy. My gynecologist informed me that my uterus was severely tilted and this may be the cause for infertility. We were baffled for awhile but I agreed to monthly observations as well as treatment that he had prescribed. The discovery of my medical problems did not affect our relationship; on the contrary, it seemed to pull us closer together. Matthew told me he had no doubt that we would have children. He made it very clear in one of our discussions.

> *No good thing will He withhold from them that walk uprightly! (Psalms 37:4)*

After a year of numerous medical treatments we were advised that I needed a corrective surgery and that it would be the best option to address my infertility. We readily agreed without even probing the pros and cons of the surgery. I think my husband was becoming desperate so he suggested adoption as our option if the surgery had failed. I was not ready to explore the possibility of adopting children but I unwillingly agreed. I wanted to conceive and have my own children. Of course I did not share my feelings with Matthew; he would have been crushed. He regularly brought over two of his god-children whom he nurtured at times and brought them home to spend time with us. My conviction was based on these words:

> *The effective, fervent prayer of a righteous man avails much. (James 5:16)*

One afternoon, after reading the section of the daily newspaper I was alerted by the article "Abundant Children". The staggering number of children that were affected and the uncertainty of these children's future moved me. I became so overwhelmed that I held the paper up and cried out to the Lord. "This is not fair God! I would have been a good mother to these children and you just refuse to give me the opportunity to have children!!" My tears were flowing, I felt wounded, hurt and sad. Why? Why? I pleaded, Jesus, if you bless me with a child, I certainly would not abandon your precious gift. My mind was cloudy, my vision blurred, my legs became weak, and my heart ached from the mental pain that I felt. Looking back now, I felt like Hanna in her desperation while seeking God's blessing for a son; God granted her the desires of her heart. In her exaltation unto the Lord, she said:

> *My heart rejoices in the Lord; my horn is exalted in the Lord. ...No one is holy like the Lord, for there is none besides You, Nor is there any rock like our God. (1Samuel 2:1-2)*

I built up my hopes that my corrective surgery would be the solution to my problem. We hastened to the University of the West Indies Medical Center to meet with my doctor. All the decisions would be finalized in this visit with my gynecologist before surgery. Both of us were happy about the progress, but there was an unexpected turn of events. My regular doctor was away from his office so another gynecologist was assigned to me. The new gynecologist examined me and reviewed my medical records carefully as well as the planned procedure that was being scheduled. He asked numerous questions as to why I wanted to do the surgery. I informed him of my five years of marriage that gone by and how much we wanted a baby. He sounded more like my counselor instead of a doctor. We both studied each other as he examined me. We spoke at length after the examination; and it appeared like he was probing me, but why? Finally he gave his advice, "You are a young woman and you need to wait on God, you don't need to rush. God will bless you in His own time." He then cautioned me before I left not to share our discussion with the medical staff especially my gynecologist. Everything about this doctor visit was strange, leaving me in a state of surprise. His stature was unusual he was little over five feet tall, soft spoken, with intense eyes that focused on me intently as well as every word that I uttered. It appeared like he was studying me carefully before he spoke.

As I journeyed home I struggled to make sense of this doctor and his directive to me. My thoughts reflected back to my grandmother's quote, "Doctors do not go against each other." Later, I checked to see who he was, where he worked, as well as where he studied medicine. I found out that he studied medicine abroad as well as in Jamaica. I wanted to know if this was what really Jesus wanted me to do. Numerous questions emerged but there were no answers. Was this a coincidence or God's plan that I had this doctor attending to me? I was perplexed, and this song was the source of my inspiration:

Teach me Lord, to wait......on my knees

Teach me, Lord to wait
Down on my knees
Till in your own good time
You will answer my pleas
Teach me not to rely on what others do
But to wait in prayer
For an answer from You

"Was this man sent by God to direct me?" I was puzzled and could not get the thought out of my mind. It was agonizing because I could not make sense of anything, which is very unusual for me. After that moment I did not know what decision to make with the impending surgery that would be within two weeks. After days of being undecided what to do, we prayed, then I decided that I would cancel the surgery and wait. Both Matthew and I suggested that I could reschedule it for another time. Days before the surgery I informed my regular gynecologist of my decision. He was stunned when I suddenly told him that I am cancelling my surgery without any real explanation. I told him we will wait for awhile. He wanted some answers as to my change of heart especially since we were desperate to have a baby. I refused to share the real source of my decision and I left his office almost in tears. I had no way of knowing if I were giving up my chance to have children. I had to rely on my faith. At that moment, I kept repeating parts of David's prayer unto the Lord. This was way of comforting my heart and believing that He would make a way somehow for me.

Wait on the LORD: be of good courage,
and he shall strengthen your heart:
Wait, I say, on the LORD.:(Psalm 27:14)

> *My help comes from the LORD,*
> *which made heaven and earth. (Psalm 121:2)*

Six months later I was constantly tired and sleepy. I decided that I needed to see the gynecologist because I could not understand the feelings I experienced. As I described my symptoms he kept on doing the usual tests. I became fearful when he kept silent for awhile. Finally, he was smiling but I was still in the dark. "Congratulations Mrs. Palmer, you are pregnant and will be a mother soon!" *Did I hear correctly?* He repeated himself. I was too elated to reply. Jubilation, disbelief, fear, excitement, took over all at once! I dashed home and shared the excellent news. Matthew was a bit quiet but extremely happy so I asked, "What is it that you are not sharing with me?"

"I knew that you were pregnant."

"What! You knew?" "Yes, I wanted the doctor to confirm it."

After much probing to uncover how he knew, he explained the signs as well as his constant observations. We worshipped God for hearing our appeals as we celebrated and waited on the arrival of our baby. It was impossible to keep quiet; my heart over flowed with joy as I rejoice in singing aloud.

> *I want to thank you Lord*
> *Thank you Lord that you ever thought of me*
> *Many are the blessings that have give unto me*
> *Blessings over-flowing like a mighty sea*
> *Lord I want to thank you for your love to me*
> *When I think of the goodness of Jesus*
> *And what He hath done for me*
> *My soul cry out Hallelujah*
> *Thank God for saving grace*

My pregnancy was without complications, I was overfilled with joy and I adorned myself in the most beautiful way. We spend hours poring over names and plans to receive our first baby. Doctor visits were constantly followed by carefully planned nutrition. Matthew took full charge of my daily routines, making sure that I followed the doctor's orders, such as daily balanced meals, intake of iron, exercise, and adequate rest. During my fifth month of pregnancy I had a strange dream that I fully ignored. In my vision my deceased mother-in-law paid me a visit. She warned me that there would be major difficulties with my delivery and gave me an instruction that I should carry out. I chased her away and reminded her that she had passed and should never show up again. I informed Matthew about it; he said that he had no fear, knowing that his mother and I had an awesome relationship during her lifetime. I had completely forgotten this dream when I entered the hospital for my delivery.

My due date had passed and although I had no problems the doctor instructed that I be admitted to the hospital to induce labor. Matthew and Mama were with me as I headed to the hospital not knowing what to expect. We all thought that I would have the baby soon. The process began early the next morning and lasted for 48 hours. It was almost fatal to both my baby and me, but the Lord was on our side.

> *Behold ye that keepeth Israel shall neither slumber nor*
> *sleep. The Lord is thy keeper: the Lord is thy shade upon*
> *thy right hand. (Psalm 121: 4-5)*

As I laid in bouts of unbearable pain while constantly enduring the regularly testing that was necessary to see the location of the baby, I tried my best to keep a positive mind. It became unbearable when I overhead a nurse saying that I was the only one that was still in labor from yesterday. I saw the concern on the matron's face as she opted to check on me herself. She sent out a distress call for the doctor to see me as early as possible. As she spoke to him on the phone she told him that the baby was in distress, the heart beat was irregular. "Oh God, please don't let us die." Within a short time my records were reviewed at a meeting with a medical team. While they decided on my fate and the next procedure that should be taken, I became fearful. Everyone was busy while an intern watched over me. I remembered him reading a story to me. My pain became so unbearable and I had no interest in his efforts of comfort. I knew that I was getting really weak and may have been going in and out of consciousness. I kept praying, and praying, knowing that I was faced with the possibility of death.

> *I sought the LORD, and he heard me, and delivered me*
> *from all my fears. (Psalm 34:4)*

Suddenly, I felt a calm presence; I looked up and I saw Matthew's mother peering over at me. The intern was shocked when he heard me speaking loudly to someone, although he did not see anyone. It was late in the night. "Mammy, Mammy," I shouted, "why are you staring at me, can't you see that I am dying, can't you do something?" She waved her hand and walked backwards and left.

The intern was so confused he could not make sense of my actions so he ran and called for help. Within a few minutes a medical team arrived. I demanded that I be taken to the delivery room. "I am ready to have my baby now," I implored. In the midst of the confusion, they agreed. By the time we got there I was a bit dazed, limp, and tired, but the baby was on a fast track ready to be delivered. There were difficulties and the doctor did a minor incision in the process, but nothing matters now; there was my baby weighing seven and a half pounds. Her proud dad named her Ann. I was told that the doctors were about to perform surgery, but I knew God took over from them. I was hardly conscious when the announcement was made, "It's a girl!" I was too weak to join in the celebration but her proud dad took over. We held hands and worshipped our Creator, 'O come let us adore him' was our theme.

At birth my daughter appeared battered and bruised, limp, but alive. The doctor told me that I was extremely lucky that the baby was alive due to the trauma that she went through. Although this hospital is a teaching institution, surgery was not decided upon readily, it had to be the final option. Looking back now, I think they had me in labor for too long and that was a threat to both lives. I can testify that it is through God's love and His grace that I can share this miracle with you. We stayed in the hospital for over a week before heading home. Ann was God's beautiful gift to us and we were ecstatic. After my recovery, I started to visualize the true meaning of these songs:

> *Have you any rivers?*
> *That you think are uncrossable*
> *Have any mountain that you can't tunnel through*
> *Yes, God specializes*
> *In things that seems impossible*
> *And He can do what no other power can do*

> *No, never alone! No, never alone!*
> *He promised never to leave me,*
> *Never to leave me alone!*
> *No, never alone! No, never alone!*
> *He promised never to leave me,*
> *Never to leave me alone!*

Mama and Matthew were regulars at the hospital; they made sure that our care was super. As I gained my strength from the two week-long ordeal, I consistently praised God for sparing our lives. I believed that I was the happiest mother in the world when I stepped out of the hospital with my baby bound for new challenges and a brighter future. At home Matthew became a full time nurse as he continued to hold on to his job. As proud parents we praised God because it is no secret what God can do and has done for me. From the beginning of her life we taught Ann about Jesus and His love. Our training was based on:

> *Train up a child in the way he should go: and when he is*
> *old he will not depart from it. (Proverbs 22:6)*

Her growth and development was amazing, and that brought lots of happiness in our home. Working with lots of children from different backgrounds gave me the ability to understand different types of behavior readily; I recognized early that her stubbornness and determination would constantly keep us on our toes. Ann was walking and talking months before her first birthday, and it was not long before she wanted a little brother. She loved outdoor activities so she was always outdoors alongside her dad and that may have contributed to her request. He took her just about everywhere with him, it did not matter if I were present or not. We taught her the word of God and how to be respectful, *honor your father and mother that your days maybe long upon the land;* she learn how to pray, and seek God's blessings. She loved attending church and she was a star in her Sunday school class.

Motherhood was like a hidden world to me and I equipped myself as best I could so that I would be an effective parent and a role model in her life. The la-la-byes were comforting but she learned words quickly so we advance to songs, Bible verses and nursery rhymes. This was a time when I started to reflect on most of the things that I learned as a child and how I would apply them with my child. Some of the poems and songs that I was taught as a child stood out so we sang them together. She had an enquiring mind that was beyond her age, so that kept us busy. Her poise and beauty stood out and she would make friends within minutes. Ann displayed leadership skills at an early age and that gave her the advantage over her peers. Her inspiration was stunning to everyone who knew her.

> *Jesus loves me this I know*
> *For the bible tells me so '*

Little ones to him belong
They are weak but he is strong
Yes Jesus loves me
Yes Jesus loves me
For the bible tells me so
&
A sunbeam a sunbeam
Jesus wants me to be a sunbeam
A sunbeam a sunbeam
I'll be a sunbeam for Him
&
Don't lean on others to be a man
Stand on a footing of her own
Be independent if you can
And cultivate a strong background

Contrary to what some people believe about training and spanking, we disciplined her, which included a few spankings, which were rare. Parents should not be fearful of disciplining their children because we were instructed by God's principles in Proverbs 22:6 to train a child up in the right way. It can be proven from our statistics that children who grow without discipline have been a menace to themselves, family, and the society as a whole. During Ann's formative years I learned a lot by watching her grow.

In my final year at Mico Teacher's College I was expecting my second child. Even though my due date had passed, I was determined not to be induced into labor a second time. I prayed and waited and refused to go to the hospital as instructed. A week later, as I prepared to attend one of my Friday morning class, I had to be rushed to Spanish Town Public Hospital where my doctor engaged in my delivery. I was considered high risk, so the team was fully alerted in case there were complications. Although, I had lost excessive amount of blood during my delivery, this was far better than my previous experience. My 10-pound son arrived into the world with haste, looking fully alert and ready to be fed. Ann was now three years old and wanted full command of her baby brother. It was an exciting time for all of us and he thrived in an unusual manner. They were very different in their manner; she was always the boss and he would follow her commands although he was unhappy about it at times. He was more of an introvert while she was the total opposite. At times she was protective of him in many ways. As he grew it was evident his intelligence was super, and he was always seeking knowledge.

I was fully convinced that we had the perfect number of children and I was fully engaged in their upbringing. Six years later I was pregnant with my third child. In my fifth month I had a miscarriage and I was miserable. I cried daily, I was fragile emotionally. I was on extended sick leave from my teaching job still grieving about the loss when the Lord spoke to me expressively. I was very sad as I sat in the living room, when I heard a voice. I was alarmed for awhile but recognized that still small voice. Jesus assured me that He would bless me. These words came to me: *The joy of the Lord is your strength*. I knew then that God wanted me to be whole so I took courage. This experience with the Holy Spirit in the time of my pain has allowed me to sing this hymn today:

There is no pain, Jesus can't feel
There is no hurt, that He cannot heal
For all things work
According to the masters purpose
And his holy will
No matter what you're are going thru,
Remember that God only wants a chance to use you
The battle its not yours
It's the Lords

There is no pain Jesus can't feel
And there is no sadness Jesus can't heal
For all things work according to the master's will
No matter what you are going through
Remember God is only using you
For battle its not yours
It's the Lords

There and then I got up and claimed my healing; Christ must know the reason for my loss. I regained my strength and returned to work with peace of mind knowing that God was in control of my life.

Three months later I was pregnant and God blessed me with my daughter Alli. I noticed a difference in her manner as well as her spirit. As she grew she had a calm spirit and was always seeking knowledge like her brother. As parents we took our responsibility as a sacred duty to rear our three children in love and righteousness, to provide for their physical and spiritual needs, to teach them to love and serve others, to observe the commandments of God and to be law-abiding citizens wherever they lived.

My three children were not accidents each was a blessing in many different ways. They are regular people, who have all excelled, and are gainfully contributing to our society and the progress of mankind. In our daily devotions I continue to thank God for His mighty works and the blessings that He has bestowed upon me. As I grew in His grace I learned that I should not worry because John the Revelator reminded me of the word of God:

> *Ye are of God, little children, and have overcome them: because greater is he that is in you, than he that is in the world. (1 John 4:4)*

I lived my life daily believing and practicing these words. He has endowed greatness in us but we must believe it to receive it. All the praise belonged to Christ who heads my life; and it is fact that he blesses me beyond measure.

> *I am blessed. I am blessed.*
> *Every day that I live, I am blessed.*
> *When I wake up in the morning,*
> *Till I lay my head to rest,*
> *I am blessed. I am blessed.*
>
> *Through the sunshine and rain,*
> *Even sorrow and pain,*
> *Jesus is still my comfort and guide.*
> *And His love comforts me,*
> *And His grace has set me free,*

Chapter 5
A New Beginning

>◇◇◇◇<

Where He may leads I will go; for I have learn to trust Him so…
Jesus shall lead me night and day; Jesus shall lead me all the way,
He is the truest Friend to me.; For I remember Calvary

This was the song that sprang up in my heart as I waited on a call from Matthew regarding our departure from Jamaica to the United States of America. What was taking him so long? "We are ready to leave, the summer will be gone before you know it and yet there were no tickets. We are tired of waiting so let's go and buy our tickets Mom," exclaimed Rick. The three tickets arrived before I could take my son's advice, so I informed them that we would be leaving within a few days. The children wasted no time in getting ready to leave. I was bombarded with questions as to what life would be in Miami for them. My explanation had prepared them for an excellent time.

It was a beautiful day as we boarded Air Jamaica for Miami. After take-off we peered through the window of the 737 airplane to view the vast stretch of land and ocean. As we approached Miami, the morning sun was shining brightly, and we could see land, it was fully occupied with buildings of every size, shape, and color. This was the children's first flight, and it lasted for about ninety minutes. As we taxied along the runway the pilot announced, "Welcome to Miami, thanks for flying with us: be careful as you continue to your destination." For my three children, Rick, Alli, and Ann the moment of jubilation was fast approaching. Nothing mattered as long as they were reunited with their daddy whom they had not seen during the last three months. We were so anxious, but we breathed a quiet prayer for our safe landing.

Everything seemed perfect as we embarked at the Miami International Airport on a hot day in the summer of 1985. We took some time as we dealt with the hassle of the immigration. Rick's brown teddy bear affection called "Brother" was the main subject of questioning and discussion. The immigration officer mangled Brother before tossing him in a garbage bin right in Rick's presence, although there were no infractions against us. The shock that went through us was alarming. We were informed later that immigration was bombarded with travelers who used their children's toys to transport illegal substances. My son was terrified; he expected me to protect his brother from this barbaric treatment. I was numbed, helpless, confused, and embarrassed knowing that the officer observed all the personal belongings in our baggage. What would cause someone to hurt a child in this manner especially when we did not break the law? Tears streamed down Rick's face as he begged for his teddy bear. I practically dragged him along when we were told that we were free to leave; he was reluctant to leave Brother" behind. He made an attempt to retrieve Brother from the garbage bin but the officer prohibited him from doing so. There were no explanations, no empathy, and that just added to our confusion. Previously, I had visited Miami and I brought gifts for my friends and there were no problems with the immigration so I had no reason to think that this behavior existed.

Brother was specially designed and handmade for him at birth by a close friend with whom I worked in a public school. My son shared every inch of his life with his teddy bear on a daily basis. At bed time he made it his duty to read a story to him and cuddled him and off they went to sleep. He dressed him in his clothes, school uniform on week days and regular clothes on the weekends. These two were inseparable so he made sure his brother was with him at every step during the journey. He wanted him to be with him at his new home in United States. There was some reassurance that they will be enjoying themselves on arrival. Rick asked permission and received a commitment from me that his brother would not be left behind. With Brother left in the garbage bin at the airport the joy of reuniting with daddy after three months of separation was subdued to a bitter-sweet experience. On our way to our new home the focus of discussion was the unexpected treatment of my son's companion.

On arrival home we began to examine our environment when someone asked, "Where is Rick?" We all got busy searching every inch of the property. He was nowhere in sight so we frantically went on the street in pairs along with friends to search for him. After thirty minutes he was found wondering along a busy street. During our interrogation of his disappearance, he stated that he was on his way to the airport to retrieve his only brother, his teddy bear. Within days I made every effort to replace Rick's teddy bear but he had refused the replacement. What would happen next? I had to comfort him as well as myself. This was not the kind of start we had anticipated. Brother's demise was unfortunate and Rick was very unhappy and wanted all of us, including his father, to return home to Jamaica as quickly as possible.

What was ahead of us! That was the thought that kept ringing in my ear. How can I regain the trust and confidence that my son had in me. Why was I unable to protect him when he needed it most? I was now stuck between *a rock and a hard place.* I did all I could to provide some solace for him but the wound was deep.

> *Come unto to me, all yet that labor and are heavy laden,*
> *and I will give you rest. (Matthew 11: 28)*

I kept repeating *The earth is the LORD'S, and the fullness thereof; the world, and they that dwell therein.* I was confident that God would take care of us. The rest of the day was spent reassuring my kids that they would start a happy life here like the one they had experienced in Jamaica or maybe it would be even better. The entire ordeal presented an atmosphere of doubt and fear for all of us.

We managed to huddle together for comfort as their dad took over. The greeting had lost some of the excitement but we were more than happy to be together after three months of separation. Long-awaited stories emerged as Ann and Alli competed for the top spot on their dad's leg, while Rick kept to himself. After awhile his dad took him for a walk just the two of them; they had a private moment. An hour later they appeared and then he tried to be a part of the celebration. After the children retired to bed that night, Matthew and I discussed several strategies that we would apply as a means to resolve his anger and ways to comfort him. It was very difficult for him during the months that followed. He has never fully overcome his loss. As a child this was the most barbaric thing that he had ever experienced.

Having to reside in an apartment for the first time with the children presented some difficulties. The sense of freedom was limited due to the change in lifestyle. In Jamaica they were able to run and play freely in the yard. They also felt threatened by the lack of privacy and rules that were enforced by the landlord. The landlord was our neighbor and their children seemed to be the privileged ones. The sudden changes unearthed a culture shock along with the change in our lifestyle.

As a teacher in Jamaica along with my husband's income we were able to provide more for them. Our limited income after our arrival in Miami in the first three to four years added to their frustration. This was the first taste of hardship for them. They were all accustomed to a housekeeper in the home and a modest lifestyle, which was considered as being middle class.

How could Mommy and Daddy give up everything and move here? We were only going to be spending the summer holiday; and now we are living here. "We want to go back to our old school," announced Rick followed by the girls' endorsements. This is not even a house it is just like a hotel. They refused to go to the nearby stores where we lived in Coconut Grove. They practically stayed indoors daily. I was tempted several times to take my children back home but I encountered a sense of fear in raising and nurturing them without their dad. I pleaded with my husband for us to return home for the sake of the children. His response was always positive. "V, God has brought us too far to fail us now."

God will never leave you nor forsake you. (Hebrews 13:5)

The journey we anticipated had been dashed and this seems like an awful experience for the children but we kept encouraging them. After my leave of absence ended, I decided that I would remain in Miami because it was in the best interest of the children. After doing some odd jobs, I was finally employed in a private school as an assistant teacher in a pre-kindergarten class. This was not well received by some staff members because I was the only African American to have been employed in this facility. The parents showed a lot of respect due to my teaching styles and the level of their children's progress within a short time. It did not take long before tension started to build between the manager and the director who had hired me, but I kept clear of it. The manager had a long-term contract with the school and lived on the premises along with her family.

One afternoon while I was tending to school matters the tension boiled over and I overheard the manager demanding the director to remove that black girl from the staff. Insults were hurled at each other and the director took a stand; she fired back at her reminding her that she was an employee as well. The director also stated that she had the authority to hire the best teachers to work for her in her school. The fight lasted for awhile and finally the director fired the manager on the spot. This was my first real encounter with race, prejudice, and its impact on my life. This was an eye opener for me. I felt out of place, I did not know what to do, I froze thinking what have I might have done to generate so much anger. I knew the Lord had encamped around me that day. I took courage in these words:

> *And the Lord, he it is that doth go before thee; he will be*
> *with thee, he will not fail thee, neither forsake thee: fear*
> *not, neither be dismayed. (Deuteronomy 31:8)*

Some staff members celebrated quietly while others stated that this was the straw that broke the camel's back. Many stated that the manager was rude, insensitive, and had a lack of concern for others. Most of the staff members had encountered difficulties with her prior to this incident so they had no sympathy for her.

As the months went by I was promoted to teach my own class and I received an increase in salary as well as more leadership responsibilities. My youngest daughter attended the school as part of my benefits. We were not in a position to pay tuition at a private school on Bayshore Drive that serves children of influential professionals. My boss was very supportive to my family and me. She assisted us in numerous ways, such as driving us home several times when we missed the bus or when it was too cold to be standing outside waiting on a bus for over an hour. My home was a long distance from the school but she took on the responsibility as much as needed. She guided me in selecting Coconut Grove Elementary School for my daughter when she had completed the private school program. It was a smooth transition and both schools provided rich experiences that extended her knowledge beyond the norm. Alli traveled extensively, participated in numerous competitions, and she was graced with presenting the Queen of England with a beautiful bouquet of flowers on one of her visits to the United States. These schools had truly prepared her for major undertakings that led her to succeed in her education.

Meanwhile I juggled work and school with the hope of making my way to the public school. Although, it was difficult, we made the best out of the situation. As I reflected on this hymn I could see how it applied to me; God has truly guided us throughout this time.

> *Life is like a mountain railroad,*
> *with an engineer that's brave;*
> *We must make the run successful,*
> *from the cradle to the grave;*
> *Watch the curves, the fills, the tunnels;*
> *never falter, never quail;*
> *Keep your hand upon the throttle, and*
> *your eye upon the rail.*

Bless'd Savior, Thou wilt guide us,
Till we reach that blissful shore;
Where the angels wait to join us
In Thy praise forevermore.

You will roll up grades of trial;
you will cross the bridge of strife;
See that Christ is your Conductor on
this evening train of life;
Always mindful of obstruction,
do your duty, never fail;
Keep your hand upon the throttle,
and your eye upon the rail.

You will often find obstructions;
look for storms of wind and rain;
On a fill, or curve, or trestle, they
will almost ditch your train;
Put your trust alone in Jesus;
never falter, never fail;
Keep your hand upon the throttle,
and your eyes upon the rail.

In the meantime, Matthew was convinced that he was at the right place; all he needed to do was wait on his blessings. "God will not leave us or forsake us," he kept reminding me. "God had shown me this place several times in my vision and I was able to identify the streets and locations when I got here, so please let us be patient," he implored. He was very humble and he showed empathy towards my concerns but remained unmoved. We knew that perseverance would be the key to our success. It felt like we were on the rough side of the mountain but we must keep fighting on. All I knew was that I was climbing up on the rough side of the mountain and I must hold on to God's powerful hand. As I climbed, sometimes my burdens pressed me down, but I was determined to succeed.

I worked hard and we managed to keep our lives together. Although the school system was new to us, good grades as well as conduct were expected and the children strived for the best. The first three years in Miami were the most difficult; I had never worked so hard or experienced so many challenges in my life before. God gave us the tools to overcome, but it was not an easy road. I had very little direction in entering my career so I ended up repeating most of my previous courses in education. Within five years I obtained an Associate of Arts, Bachelors of Arts in Elementary Education, and a Master's Degree in Guidance Counseling. Later on, I tried to resist the urge of a doctoral degree but I went on studying and graduated with a Doctor of Philosophy in Mathematics. I had overcome major obstacles but my church, as well as some good Samaritans assisted me before I was gainfully employed by Dade County Public Schools. I am convinced that I could not have made these accomplishments on my own, it was God. The commitment that I made to Him has brought about abundance of benefits and blessings.

> *Commit thy way unto the LORD; trust also in him; and*
> *he shall bring it to pass.(Psalm 37:5)*

Once I had an unpleasant experience with an administrator who tried to block one of my internships. My pleas were ignored, and I finally enlightened her with the authority that is given to me:

> *No good thing does the Lord withhold from those who*
> *walk uprightly.(Psalm 84:11)*

I told her in a polite manner that God said to me, "Velma Palmer, no good thing will I withhold from you, so you cannot stop my progress." I tried to take a leave of absence but I was ineligible for it, so that failed as well. As a last resort my administrator encouraged me to resign from my job but that was not an option. Lord you have to take care of me because you have promised me that you will never leave me or forsake me.

My internship lagged behind for months while my classmates were all settled and practicing counseling at several locations. I was the only one left out in the cold. My college professors kept calling me wanting to know what they could do to assist me, but they were unable to resolve this matter. It was not approved by my administration and I was convinced that it was all out of spite. The college had no choice, but to inform me that my cancellation from the program was approaching within days. I was worried and angry, after spending thousands of dollars on a degree that I would not complete. I sought the Lord and He heard me. The Holy Spirit urged me to go to the internship. How could this be, I needed nine months to attend. My spirit was quickened, and a voice spoke, "Velma, go to the internship tomorrow." I tossed all night, although it seemed hopeless, I obeyed.

I was scared but I gained strength as I echoed, "Jesus Savior pilot me," while I was on my way. My supervisor was elated to see me; she greeted me like a friend who hadn't seen each other in a long time. She wasted no time in preparing me to counsel different small groups within the school. My supervisor's statement encouraged me; she stated that we belong to the same Father. "I knew you would come, so I kept praying and waiting." She was unaware of my struggles, but I knew God was working on my behalf. As we sat down for lunch, she wanted an answer as to my whereabouts during the past five weeks of absence. I was nervous, embarrassed, and afraid, but I explained what had happened, and I that I may not be able to complete the internship. I informed her that I would only be there for a few visits because my administrator did not approve me for any time. She immediately sought approval at a higher level and it was granted along with a schedule that accommodated me in the after school program. It was ironic that when my supervisor made the call, both of our bosses were in attendance at the same meeting. My administrator had a family emergency so there was no time to discuss my situation. I was free to move forward with my internship. This was a special approval and she supervised me throughout that year, four afternoons per week without being paid. As a result of my late start, my attendance had to be increased. My supervisor whom I have never met before was as determined as I was for me to succeed. I was able to complete my internship with excellent grades, and graduated with my classmates. My Lord has never failed me yet!

> *The LORD is my rock, and my fortress, and my deliverer;*
> *My God, my strength, in whom I will trust; my buckler,*
> *and the horn of my salvation, and my high tower.(*
> *Psalm18:2)*

It took years before my three children became well adjusted to their new country and the way of life. As they grew and studied, they made major successes. All three children have graduated from college with degrees in Elementary Education, Business Administration, and Mechanical Engineering. The reality of their success is a direct result of the worth of prayer. The foundation of our lives is built on prayer and even when we are confronted with obstacles or sometimes down-trodden we continue praying and waiting on our deliverance. When the children complained about their difficulties in school or in general we laid our hands on them and prayed and informed them that God will resolve it. I praise God for His abundant blessings to me throughout my life. I join with David when he expressed how he could never repay God for His goodness towards him.

> *What shall I render unto the LORD for all his benefits*
> *toward me? (Psalm 116:12)*

My experience left me rejoicing as I praise God in sing:

> *Great is thy faithfulness, O God my Father;*
> *There is no shadow of turning with thee;*
> *Thou changest not, thy compassions, they fail not;*
> *As thou hast been thou forever will be.*
>
> *Great is thy faithfulness! Great is thy faithfulness!*
> *Morning by morning new mercies I see;*
> *All I have needed thy hand hath provided;*
> *Great is thy faithfulness, Lord, unto me!*

One year after our arrival, summer 1986.

Chapter 6
Never Give Up

><><

*Wait on the LORD: be of good courage, and he shall strengthen
thine heart: wait, I say, on the LORD   (Psalm 27:14)*

The journey had just begun! My new home and life presented major
challenges. My previous achievement in the teaching profession seemed
worthless because of the new requirements in the United States. There was
very little direction so I quickly realized that I had to start my professional
career all over. Having reached a comfortable position in my professional
life, then realizing that I had nothing made me cry many times. I was very
frustrated with the low paying jobs that I acquired and I was determined
to change my status. I have never experienced this level of employment
before; it was new to me. I had to work much harder than I could ever
remember in my life.

I made several attempts to have my college transcript from Mico
Teacher's College assesses but each time I was told that the person who was
responsible for the assessment at Florida International University (FIU)
was unavailable. I got frustrated and decide to forget the transcript and
start college from *scratch*. My prayer was made know unto the Lord.

*Delight yourself also in the LORD; and he shall give you
the desires of your heart. (Psalm 37:4)*

I made a pledge to rise above these obstacles by attending college and
securing a four-year degree. After discussing my plans with my family
I enrolled in Miami Dade Community College. After examining the
program in elementary education, I realized that it would be difficult due
to my eight to nine hours of daily employment as well as attending classes
four nights weekly and on Saturdays.

I had no one to direct me in the process of college entry so I started out
in some remedial classes and some unnecessary courses that were foreign
to me. One course that still lingers in my mind is college survival. It had
nothing to offer me and was a complete waste of money but I had no way

of knowing due to the lack of educational advising. I was worried that it would take ages for me to complete a degree because of the basic courses that were being selected for me. The comfort zone I once knew did not exist anymore and I had to fight my way through. Looking back, I view this situation as brutal; I had to work night and day for our survival.

This adjustment was extremely difficult for all of us especially my children, but I had to go forward. My determination grew as I selected the classes. "We will not live like this, I must succeed," I assured the family. Securing a degree in the profession that I loved and was fully versed in would be our only escape from poverty, so I proceeded with full speed. Within two weeks all my professors concluded that I should not be in their classes, I was too advanced. I was removed from two of the remedial classes to regular classes but I had to keep the third remedial class. All I did was to believe that Christ would make a way, so I kept on trusting in Him.

> *Trust in the Lord with all thine heart; and lean not unto thine own understanding. In all thy ways acknowledge him, and he will direct your paths straight. (Proverbs 3:5-6)*

My desperation led me to increase my course load from twelve credit hours to eighteen credit hours. My husband and I, professionals in Jamaica, were now practically working for minimum wage, so paying for college, and maintaining a family of five was a major challenge. But I kept encouraging myself with the words:

> *But my God shall supply all your need according to his riches in glory by Christ Jesus. (Philippians 4:19)*

I had four major set-backs during my attendance at college that could have totally derailed me. My father passed away and I was unable to attend his funeral due to immigration matters; I lost my job due to bankruptcy of the school; my daughter was in a coma for weeks due to a near drowning incident, followed by my husband's major accident that affected him severely and left him without employment for several years. These trials took their toll on me but I remained afloat because of God's love towards me. These set-backs lead me to maintain a closer relationship with God. This gave me the opportunity to:

> *Cast your burden on the Lord and he shall sustain thee:*

> *He shall never suffer the righteous to be moved. (Psalm 55:22)*

We single-handedly paid for all the classes so we survived on a strict budget. The children were unaccustomed to this life-style so they demanded some answers from us as to the changes. Matthew took on total responsibility of running the home while I pushed myself forward. At work and at home I used every opportunity to study, even at restroom breaks. Amidst my struggles while coping with major illnesses, lack of finance, family matters including college, I managed to maintain a grade point average over of 3.0. This was considered serious juggling because Matthew was not able to drive due to his medical condition, so I had to chauffeur the family to appointments, school, grocery shopping, and church, which was overwhelming. During this time, I remembered one great lesson that is found in this chorus:

> *Put your hands in the hands of the man who stilled the water*
> *Put your hands in the hands of the man who calmed the seas*
> *Take a look at yourself and you can look at others differently*
> *Put your hands in the hands of the man from Galilee*

During my final semester in college I had an unusual experience. Final exams were completed and I failed my algebra class. This set off an alarm in my head, "This is not possible I kept saying to myself. I had a "B" average in the class, so I could not have failed." I was sad and was not sure how I would handle the situation. I knew college would be closed for the break and I may not even see my professor again.

While I was home cooking on the final day of closing I had an urge from the Lord *Go to Miami-Dade Community College.* "Why," I whispered. I just could not escape the push. Finally, I asked my husband to take over the cooking, "I will be back soon." "What's wrong," he enquired. "I'll let you know when I get back," I said. I quickly washed my hands, picked up two dollar bills and put them into my pocket; he stared as I left in a hurry.

I raced to the first train heading downtown, without even my pocket book. I really did not know why the Holy Spirit wanted me to go there, but I decided on the train that my mission was to ask my professor to review my grades. I arrived at my classroom close to seven o'clock. I peered in looking for my professor; it was quiet and I saw six of my classmates re-taking their algebra test. He was away from the room but within a few minutes he arrived. Now, I knew why the Lord had to literally drag me down here. I requested to speak to him but he was unwilling to see me. However, he complied after I insisted, "I was the one with the highest score in your mathematics class and I don't see how I failed the exam. Why are these students re-taking the exam?" Secondly, if any one should be invited to do a retake the exam, I should be one of them. He protested so I informed him that I would get the dean involved. He was more than willing for me to re-take it at that juncture; he also did not want the re-takers to know what was going on. I could see that he was nervous and I wasted no time in making my demands. I pointed out that it was already after seven o'clock and I could not finish a test in such a short time; the college will be closing the doors at eight o'clock. "I will wait on you no matter how long you take to complete your test," he said.

I was not prepared. I had no pen or pencils, so he offered me two pencils. At this point I told him that I had passed the exam originally, but I would agree to retake the exam on one condition. "What is the condition?" he enquired "The exam must be graded immediately after I have completed it, entered in the database, and my grade be given to me on the spot." He agreed to my terms and we both sat there for a while. I had to pray and ask God to guide me and get me in the right frame of mind to take the new algebra test. I knew that this was unfair to me however I had very little choice. I could have waited until college resumed and made a written appeal but that was not an option at this point. Everyone completed their test and left me there, but I kept working on the problems. After completion, I waited on him as he carried out my request. I thanked him as I walked out smiling with my well-earned 'B'. I can strongly attest to Psalm 96:4:

> *For great is the LORD and greatly to be praised; He is*
> *to be feared above all gods.*

All my family activities occurred in different parts of the county, so that added to my burden. There were times when I could not recall how I got home although I was the driver of my old Mazda; I was too exhausted to recall the trips. I told Matthew that I believed that it was the Holy Spirit that took me home safely. Many times I was too tired to even eat, but I would make sure the children's homework was accounted for. First, our faith followed by education was considered top priority in our home and no one had a free pass. I explained Solomon's instruction to children concerning the importance of them learning and extending their knowledge.

Wisdom is the principal thing; therefore get wisdom: and
with all your getting get understanding. (Proverbs 4:7)

"Daddy, why do you have to take us to the park all the time," my youngest daughter enquired. She was unable to comprehend what had happen to us financially, physically and psychologically. Her siblings were older but they too were feeling the pressure but they tried to understand. They had missed having me share in their daily activities, as I would normally do before. "Mummy, when will you ever take us shopping?"

"Just be patient, I promised I'll take all of you when I graduate." I kept my promise after graduation. We went on a "shop til you drop" spree, the day was filled with excitement and overdue treats.

In less than four years I graduated from both Miami-Dade Community College and Nova Southeastern University with an Associate and a Bachelors Degree. My achievements were grounded in prayer, fasting, and hard work. I am still thanking God for the experiences that lead me through those difficulties.

Through many dangers, toils and snares...I have already come.
'Tis Grace that brought us safe thus far...
and Grace will lead us home.

The Lord has promised good to me...
His word my hope secures.
He will my shield and portion be... as long as life endures.

Graduation, Master's Degree (left) and my doctoral degree.

Weeks later I obtained a raise on my meager salary but my goal was to seek new employment that would pay higher wages as well as allow me to return to a public school system. As I continued in my old job I became unhappy when my director suddenly shifted my work hours to a later time. Lord, please help me, but I remember the lyrics of:

> *I'm under the rock, the rock is higher than I*
> *Jehovah guides me, I'm under the rock*
> *Go tell my enemy*
> *I'm under the rock Jehovah guides me*
> *Jehovah guides me, I'm under the rock*

This incident was what prompted me to move forward, so I went directly to the Dade County Public School Board and enquired about an 'aged' application that I had submitted. The person who spoke with me initially assured me that she would do her best to locate my old application. It was activated, and I was invited to visit the office the following day. All my interviews and tests were done in one day. This was not the normal procedure so I was puzzled at the speed in which things were moving. The interviewer called a principal and informed her that she had found the perfect individual for her, based on her request. It was late that afternoon but the principal had no intention of delaying. She requested that I come to the school that afternoon. Not driving downtown for the interview due to major road construction limited my ability to travel to Miami Beach that day. The principal refused to take no for an answer so she carefully pointed out the bus route that I should take to the school. The two administrators waited for me to arrive long after their working hours. They were delighted to interview me; I was hired immediately after their interview. Although, the hiring process has always taken a much longer time in the past, I was granted employment on the spot and I knew that my Savior was in control.

> *O give thanks unto the Lord for His good for his mercies endured forever. (Psalm 118:1)*

Several times He turns around the worst situations in my life for my good. This is why we should give thanks in all situations because there may be a blessing waiting for you. I acknowledge His blessings in these verses:

> *I will lift up my eyes to the hills, from where comes my help. My help cometh from the Lord who maketh heaven and earth. (Psalm 121:1-2)*

Two years later I was back in school again seeking a Master's Degree. I wanted to be versed in all the psychological aspects of child development and growth. I attended college mainly on weekends. Statistics was my major concern but I succeeded through prayer. After my internship my family and I celebrated my graduation. It was a victory won especially knowing that I was almost prevented from doing my internship. I graduated with a Master's Degree in Guidance and Counseling. My successes prove that God is real.

> *The step of a good man is ordered by the Lord and He delighted in his ways. Thou he fall he shall not utterly cast down for the Lord uphold him with his hands. (Psalms 37:23-24)*

I considered that this was the end of the rope for me concerning studying, but it seems like I reverted to my original goal. I finally convinced myself that I had done enough. What was very unusual about this is that

I was always looking into doctoral programs. I was attending a workshop when the topic emerged and a friend encouraged me to pursue it. She spent hours explaining why she thought I should register in the program.

After some discussion with my husband, he convinced me to go for it. I was skeptical about the tuition, but he reminded me of our source. I finally registered in the doctoral program at Curtin University of Technology. It was difficult especially collecting and analyzing data. The university provided excellent support along with my supervisors. As I progressed I dropped out of the program due to my workload with local government, my profession, my family as well as two children in college. One of my daughters reminded me that I would not allow any of them to quit school. I had to practice what I preached so I re-enrolled. Three times I withdrew during my eight years of study but my family and my supervisor would not let me have any peace. He actually forced the issue so that I could have my work reviewed by The American Educational Research Association on time. My inner mind was torn about it so I told myself that I couldn't afford to pay for it. The Lord knew my scheme and He made provisions that were more than what I needed to pay for the courses. Just when I was ready to pick up the pieces, I was faced with a new challenge. I received an outstanding bill from the university as well as additional courses for the degree that placed me in a different category. I disagreed with the fines so I spent days reviewing all agreements and financial statements. Students who enrolled in the program in early 2000 were locked in a lower payment than students who began their program three years later. Even if I had decided to drop the program I was required to pay the outstanding bill. It was a difficult time trying to prove that I was not liable for this payment. "Lord please lead me out of this situation," I pleaded. Days later, I found the documents that I had signed with the university in 2002 that would prove my innocence. It took some time and effort to appeal and dispute their decision although I had my original agreement sent in to them. Finally, after numerous committee meetings, the College Board gave the green light. I would be allowed to pay the old fee and the outstanding balance for previous years was dropped. I was not required to do any additional courses than what was previously stated. I was delighted to see how Christ fought my battle. Although, I lacked patience at times, I am reminded that I need to exercise these qualities:

> *Rejoicing in hope; patient in tribulation; constant in prayer. (Romans 12:12)*

> *Thou will keep him in perfect peace, whose mind is stayed*
> *on thee: because he trusts in thee. (Isaiah 26:3)*

I felt like I could not get away from school especially after my supervisor pointed out that I had completed so much work, and spent a lot of money in the program. I was caught between "a rock and a hard place" as my grandmother would say in a situation like this. What was certain was God was real to me:

> *Real, real, real He's so real to me,*
> *I love him and he gives me the victory.*
> *Many people doubt him, but I can't do without him,*
> *That is why I love him so, he's so real to me.*

"I know that you are tired V but please hang on, I will take care of most of your other responsibilities in the home," Matthew urged. My supervisor was so happy when I returned that he would not allow me to breathe, just in case I decided to leave again. I worked endlessly to complete my work. It was a long battle, I spent long hours doing research night and day. I finally saw the light at the end of the tunnel when I walked across the stage and accepted my degree. I stood tall when the announcement was made: Dr. Velma Palmer, Doctor of Philosophy in Mathematics. I was assured on that day that:

> *With men it is impossible, but not with God: for with*
> *God all things are possible. (Mark 10:27)*

Was this real; yes it was real. This is what God has done for me and He is able to do even more for you--if you only believe. The main reason for another victory during my journey can be explained in this song:

> *Each step I take my Saviour goes before me,*
> *And with His loving hand He leads the way,*
> *And with each breath I whisper "I adore Thee;"*
> *Oh, what joy to walk with Him each day.*

> *Each step I take I know that He will guide me;*
> *To higher ground He ever leads me on.*
> *Until some day the last step will be taken.*
> *Each step I take just leads me closer home.*

> *At times I feel my faith begin to waver,*

When up ahead I see a chasm wide.
It's then I turn and look up to my Saviour,
I am strong when He is by my side.

Several times I could have given up, but I have somebody with me who bears my heavy load. It is not me but Christ that lives in me.

Chapter 7
Tragedy Strikes

><><><

For I am persuaded that neither death, nor life, nor angels, nor
principalities, nor powers, nor things present, nor things to come, nor
height nor depth, nor any other creature, shall be able to separate us from
the love of God, which is in Christ Jesus our Lord. (Romans 8:38-39)

I was awakened early that Saturday morning in the summer of` 1986 to the
sound of Matthew's trembling voice. "V--V, I think you should cancel this
trip because I had a troubling dream this morning. I dreamt that we were
all at the beach swimming and Ann drowned right in front of us, I tried to
help her but I couldn't get to her." My three children and I had anticipated
the excitement of our first beach picnic in Miami. The event was planned
by the Youth Department of the Church of God of Prophecy in Coconut
Grove. I tried to calm his apprehensions. I told him that the children
had waited for such a long time to go on this trip and they are looking
forward to have fun with the other children so I thought they should go.
My children were dealing with the separation from friends and family,
living in a new county while learning how to adapt to different cultures.
To add to their pain, their peers at school did not accept them. They were
too white for some and too black for others, so this was a difficult time
for the family. My three children were confident that they would establish
new friendships at the park.

My husband Matthew was so concerned because he said that God
showed him the danger that lies ahead in his vision. I assured him that I
would be there to protect them so don't be worried, just pray for us. He
prayed but he was still in disagreement with my decision to go to the beach.
Finally, he decided that he would stay home and prepare dinner for our
return. Although, my husband and I have always been in close contact with
the Holy Spirit, I was willing to take the children without his support for
the sake of their happiness. This was not the norm in our household; we
always worked together in making decisions for the family. Here it was
evident that my determination was contrary to what I have learned.

> *Trust in the Lord with all thine heart; and lean not on thine own understanding. In all thy ways acknowledge Him, and He shall direct thy paths. Be not wise in thine own eyes: fear the Lord and depart from evil." (Proverbs 3:5-7)*

Many cheerful children gathered at the church along with the pastor and some chaperones that were part of the fellowship. Seeing that this was our first picnic with our church, we carefully listened to all the instructions especially knowing that my children were unable to swim at that time. A dedicated member of the church drove us to Crandon Park Beach, and we arrived at the beach about 10:00 a.m. that Saturday morning. Immediately, the children raced to the ocean and the excitement was evident all around. Most of the adults included myself did not go for a swim instead we started to prepare different areas for the lunches. We were some distance from the water so we could not assist in the water activities.

I assisted with the lunch preparation, which consisted of different types of sandwiches, juices and fruits. Within two hours, lunch was ready.

Suddenly, I heard a barrage of sirens entering the beach from all directions, there were ambulances followed by a helicopter. The beach environment was suddenly transformed from fun into panic. A strange feeling came over me as I recalled the discussion I had with Matthew that morning. I suddenly became worried knowing that the children were swimming so I hurried in direction of the crowd. My strange feeling started to turn into fear; I wondered what was happening. It was necessary to comfort myself as I tried to hurry along:

> *For God has not given us the spirit of fear; but of power, and of love, and of a sound mind. (2 Timothy 1:7)*

I ran in the direction of the crowd, the weight of the sand had limited my mobility. People flooded the area but before I could make sense of the chaos, a boy who came with us on trip recognized me. As he approached me, he was almost breathless as he shouted, "Mrs. Palmer! Your daughter Ann is dead! She drowned and washed away! " I felt an extra surge of energy drain from my body, it was gone, my feet refuse to take my body and the weight of the sand held me bound. I tried frantically to move forward and through the crowd, but I was unsuccessful so someone held my hand and led me to the scene. I think for awhile, I was knocked from my senses, but the incident was all real. The paramedics' presence was seen everywhere as they worked hard to save my 14 year old daughter's life. I rambled as the paramedics asked me for her personal information. My mind was in a fog as I watched the proceedings. Both Matthew and I had made commitments to God on the basis of Him blessing us with a child, and now this could not be happening.

> *For the which cause I also suffer these things: nevertheless I am not ashamed: for I know whom I have believed, and am persuaded that he is able to keep that which I have committed unto him against that day. (2 Timothy 1:12)*

I was told by the children who were present that the incident took place while Ann was playing with a girl in the water. The girl held Ann's head under water, she resisted but the girl continued to hold her head down claiming it was a game. By the time Ann plucked herself from the girl's grip, an entire patched of her hair was left in the girl's hand. Ann was carried away by the current, and had been washed out in murky water. The lifeguard tried to jump into action but the boat refused to start. It was a race against time. Finally, a boat started and the search was intensified. She was already under water for ten minutes--too long to survive.

> *Surely he will save you from the fowler's snare and from the deadly pestilence. (Psalm 91:3)*

The girl who held Ann's head under water was a stranger to us. She was from the Bahamas visiting her aunt, a member of the church. Her aunt sent her along on the trip. After the incident she disappeared and everyone became tight-lipped. Even today, no one has ever mentioned her name or taken responsibility for her actions. It was unbelievable how no one offered any form of assistance to us knowing that we were not able financially to cope with the expenses. Christ in His mercy took us through. We have never focused on the hurt, because Christ teaches us to forgive.

> *And forgive us our trespasses, as we forgive them that trespass against us. (St. Luke 11:4)*

> *Thy word is a lamp unto my feet, and a light unto my path. (Psalm 119:105)*

We had moved from Jamaica a year prior to the incident, so we were unaware of how the legal system worked. At that moment, all we could think of was the life of our daughter Ann, although death was hanging over her head.

I watched as her limp body that was brought to shore, she was stretched out on the beach. Everyone was busy, the medical team worked desperately to pump the water out of her 14 year old, long, limp body. They did everything possible to save her life. While forcing to get her mouth open some of her upper front teeth were knocked out. The scene was grim; there was a feeling of fear, sorrow, crying, while people looked on in panic. My emotion was uncontrollable while the paramedic probed me about her personal information. After the questioning they informed me that there were no pulse but they were going to air-lift her to the hospital. There was a disagreement among the medical team as to where she should be taken. Some wanted the near-by Mercy private hospital while others selected Jackson Memorial a public hospital. The latter was selected due to the hospital's high rate of successes with trauma. Due to my emotional state I was prohibited from riding in the helicopter with my daughter. I was driven by a friend to the hospital. When I arrived, it was almost impossible to see what was being done; the small room was filled with doctors and nurses working desperately to save her life. I was convinced that God would show up and in my heart the words came alive.

> *God is our refuge and strength, a very present help in trouble. (Psalm 46:1)*

Certainly, we were in trouble. Twice she was declared dead but fought back while the doctors kept pumping and shocking her with a medical shock machine.

After a long wait, two doctors emerged with blank faces. All eyes were fastened on them; one introduced herself as the leading physician. She requested to speak to the family; our nerves shivered. She began by saying, "Ann is a fighter but it would take a miracle from God for her to live, and if she makes it she would be brain dead, just a total vegetable." Silence fell over us; we took charge immediately by holding hands as we prayed sincerely to God as never before. Tears flowed freely from everyone as our minister reminded us that God will never fail and by His stripes we are healed, God is always on time. We sang quietly:

> *He's an on time God, yes He is*
> *Job said, He may not come when you want Him*

> *But He'll be there right on time*
> *I tell you, He's an on time God, yes He is*

We believed and we sought a miracle at that very moment. It was unexplainable but I felt a sudden peace and I knew that the spirit of God was at work.

Hours later another doctor appeared and informed us that they managed to stabilize her but her lungs had collapsed, she had a serious attack of pneumonia, there was no oxygen in her blood, and they had to continue drawing water from her body. At this point she was barely clinging on to life. He explained how the salt water had completely ruined her body and that she was placed on the most critical list. I walked over to her cautiously and her eyes were completely out of the socket due to the length of time that she was under water. My pastor and I were the first ones to see her after admission. Her eyes laid lifeless on her face as we stared down on her. She was hooked up to several machines; several tubes were also attached in her throat and nose. Later her dad arrived and he was unable to cope, he broke down in tears. At this point the doctors prepared us for the worst. This scene was grim but I had hope; the words of David came alive in my heart.

> *Even, though I walk through the valley of the shadow of*
> *death, I will fear no evil: for thou art with me; thy rod*
> *and thy staff they comfort me. (Psalms 23:4)*

I arrived home late that night and I had to confront myself and decide how I was going to survive. I was mentally and physically drained. I started to reflect on the past and it appeared like a scroll, it began to roll with my entire life on it. I had prayed so much to have a baby after five years of marriage. I even reasoned with the Lord about how he gave others children that they don't need and as a result the children are classified as unwanted. I held up the newspaper to probe my point and went as far as to say that it was not right. A number of medical procedures failed to produce any offspring. Finally, I ended up with a gynecologist who informed me that I should go home and wait on God. This was an unexpected recommendation coming from a doctor but I accepted it and thanked him. I left his office with a new determination to wait on God.

> *I'm learning to lean, learning to lean,*

Learning to lean on Jesus.
Finding more power than I'd ever dreamed
Learning to lean on Jesus

A few months later I was ecstatic when my doctor told me that I was pregnant. My pregnancy followed the birth of a healthy girl baby who was received with insurmountable joy. My deliverance came only when I started to put total confidence in God as I learn to lean on Him.

For the LORD God is a sun and shield: the LORD will
give grace and glory: no good thing will he withhold from
them that walk uprightly. (Psalm 84:11)

God blessed us in a special way by giving us Ann. I could remember saying, "Please God please spare her and give her back to us. I can't take care of a brain-dead child." I don't think I comprehended the severity of being brain-dead. Questions flooded my mind. Does this really mean death or just some organs of the body unable to function normally? I was in a state of shock but I kept repeating the same prayer hoping for an instant miracle. Based on the doctor's advice, slowly I started to collect my wits as I made plans in my mind for her funeral. Pink was to be the color of her funeral since it was her favorite color.

Suddenly, I jumped to my feet and spoke loudly to myself, "I will not give up!" It was comforting as I bellowed my favorite hymn. I felt God's presence, deliverance, and peace within my heart as I moved from one stanza to the other. I was totally lost in God's love.

I must have the Savior with me,
For I dare not go alone,
I must feel His presence near me,
And His arm around me thrown.

Then my soul shall fear no ill, Let Him lead me where He will,
I will go without a murmur,
And His footsteps follow still.

I must have the Savior with me,
For my faith, at best, is weak;
He can whisper words of comfort,
That no other voice can speak,

I must have the Savior with me,
In the onward march of life,
Through the tempest and the sunshine,
Through the battle and the strife.

I must have the Savior with me,
And His eye the way must guide,
Till I reach the vale of Jordan,
Till I cross the rolling tide.

I reminded myself that power is in the name of Jesus as the tears streamed down my face. John the Apostle relates to the peace I was experiencing during the storm in my life. I found comfort in His words just like Christ disciples during His departure.

Peace I leave with you, my peace I give unto you:
not as the world giveth, give I unto you. Let not your
heart be troubled, neither let it be afraid.

I love singing, I jumped to another song seeking comfort and I was fully engrossed.

Master, the tempest is raging!
The billows are tossing high!
The sky is o'ershadow with blackness,
No shelter or help is nigh;
Carest Thou not that we perish?
How canst Thou lie asleep,
When each moment so madly is threatening
A grave in the angry deep?

The winds and the waves shall obey Thy will,
Peace, be still! Peace, be still!
They all shall sweetly obey Thy will,
Peace, peace, be still!

Whether the wrath of the storm tossed sea,
Or demons or men, or whatever it be
No waters can swallow the ship where lies
The Master of ocean, and earth, and skies;
They all shall sweetly obey Thy will,

Peace, be still! Peace, be still!
They all shall sweetly obey Thy will,
Peace, peace, be still!

I had no intention of giving up instead I used the tools that I could depend on: prayer, fasting, singing, and the word of God. Facing this critical decision was like finding myself in the mouth of a lion ready to be devoured, but still hoping he will set me free. Here I had only one source to depend on and that was found in God's love and mercy. I came to the conclusion that I am protected as stated by the Psalmist David

I shall not die but live and declare the words of the Lord.
(Psalm 118:7)

It is almost impossible to describe the inner pain that the family endured while looking at Ann's limp body. Her eye-balls hung on her face and it was protected by a shade over her face. Her dad almost collapsed at the sight of his daughter the first time we were permitted to see her in the intensive care. It was a heart wrenching experience especially, since he had forewarned me of danger. Matthew did not blame me; he reminded me that we must obey God at all times. Every day was a challenge; we were charting unknown waters but we had confidence in God. He made it clear that He will never leave us comfortless. Although I was devastated sitting in her hospital room days and nights, I took comfort in God's word and some great hymns such as:

Have you any river that seems uncrossable
Have you any mountains that you cannot tunnel through
God specializes in things that are impossible
And He will do what no other power can do

A concerned parent called me during this time of our storm and encouraged me as well as directed me to talk, sing, and read to Ann as much as possible while she lay in the hospital in a comma. She further explained that eventually your child would follow your voice back to you. The hospital became my home as I spend hours praying, singing, and reading the bible to her. Every day I sang her favorite song twice to her followed by many others:

One Day at a Time, Sweet Jesus:
I'm only human, I'm just a woman

Help me believe in what I could be
And all that I am
Show me the stairway,
I have to climb
Lord for thy sake, teach me to take
One day at a time

One day at a time sweet Jesus
That's all I'm asking from you
Just give me the strength
To do everyday what I have to do
Yesterday is gone sweet Jesus
And tomorrow may never be mine
Lord help me today, show me the way
One day at a time

One day during my singing, as she laid in Intensive Care Unit (ICU), I looked down on her and I saw some movements. Her movements did not appear random; it seemed as if she were following the rhythm of the song. I said, "Ann if you can hear me wiggle your toes." She did several times. I informed her doctor about what had transpired and he was not thrilled about my discovery. He informed me that what I saw were reflexes, not real physical movements. Although I was forewarned about her condition, I was certain that she was not brain dead as the doctors would want me to believe. I was communicating with a higher power who assured me otherwise and I would continue to believe in divine healing. Isaiah 53:5 gave me this assurance:

> *But he was wounded for our transgressions, he was*
> *bruised for our iniquities: the chastisement of our peace*
> *was upon him; and with his stripes we are healed.*

While she was in a vegetative state, I kept communicating with her in my own way as I waited on the Lord for His divine healing. Some waited patiently while others were convinced that it was over. The tide shifted, as there were discussions about the possibility of removing her life support.

One night, I had to go home to check on my family and retrieve some personal items that were needed at the hospital. With the ordeal and the stress on my body I fell asleep at home. My phone rang; I jumped up and grabbed the phone, "Mrs. Palmer this is your daughter's doctor, we need you to come back to the hospital right away." My reaction to the call led the doctor to provide some explanation; he detected that I was frightened based on the Ann's condition. "This is a miracle; Ann is awake, and the only thing that she does not know is the name of the hospital that she is in presently. She explained the ordeal to us and she also identified herself and her family's individual names." I stood up and praised God as never before.

> *Thou my everlasting portion,*
> *More than friend or life to me,*
> *All along my pilgrim journey,*
> *Savior, let me walk with thee.*
> *Close to thee, close to thee,*
> *Close to thee, close to thee,*
> *All along my pilgrim journey,*
> *Savior, let me walk with thee.*
> *&*
> *My God is an awesome God*
> *He reigns from heaven above*
> *With wings some power and love*
> *Our God is an awesome god*

I arrived at Jackson Memorial Hospital after midnight to be greeted by a team of doctors and nurses who was stunned but ecstatic. It was very difficult but a joyous experience for my family and me. I am more than grateful to them, seeing how they have worked endlessly even when my daughter's medical prognosis' was hopeless. It was amazing to see how people were "moved" by God's power. Ann progressed as she gained her strength, her sight was being restored and her mobility was remarkable. Although, she was still weak she was moved to a regular room. Her room was always busy; people were still praying and rejoicing for the victory. I was informed that throughout the ordeal friends and family established prayer groups locally and overseas to pray on my daughter's behalf. Many people told me that I was very strong because they could not handle it the way I did. This experience gave me the assurance to agree with the Apostle Paul.

> *And he said to me, My grace is sufficient for you, for my*
> *strength is made perfect in weakness. (2 Corinthians*
> *12:9)*

My family and I waited for this miracle for weeks, and this came as a surprise to the medical community, but not to us. They were unable to explain it but I knew what God had done; He took over what they could not do. Although, she was twice declared dead by the hospital she walked out on her own. This song was a testimony of the miracle seen by everyone:

It is no secret what God can do
What He's done for others, He'll do for you
With arms wide open, He'll pardon you
It is no secret what God can do.

The chimes of time ring out the news
Another day is through
Someone slipped and fell
Was that someone you?
You may have longed for added strength
Your courage to renew
Do not be disheartened
For I have news for you
There is no power that can conquer you
While God is on your side
Take Him at His promise
Don't run away and hide.
For it is no secret what God can do
What He's done for others, He'll do for you

There is no night for in His light
You never walk alone
Always feel at home
Wherever you may go.

For it is no secret what God can do
What He's done for others, He'll do for you
It is no secret what God can do.

Within days Ann started to enquire about everything. She directed most of her questions to the doctors and nurses. She also wanted detailed updates of the family activities. The day finally arrived; she was discharged from the hospital and her homecoming was greeted with celebrations. After weeks at home under the care of her doctors, they finally gave her the green light to return to school and she was elated. Chronic leg pain and headaches took its toll on her. Numerous medications and medical procedures failed to resolve the problems. Due to the difficulties and the life and death situation, her doctors had to use the veins in her feet during her treatments. They ended up being severely damaged. One of her doctors recommended a risky procedure that involved using nuclear medicine. We attended a session with the doctor, and he discussed the risk that is associated with the new procedure. He also stated that this would be the only hope to correct the damage nerves in her feet. I signed the consent then watched her wheeled into a large machine. Matthew and I kept praying, nervous but confident as we hummed silently:

> *We've come this far by faith*
> *Leaning on the Lord*
> *Trusting in His Holy word*
> *He never failed me yet*
> *Oh' Can't Turn Around*
> *We've come this far by faith …*

After the procedure ended, we knew that we had to wait for days to see the result. Within two weeks the pain subsided and then it finally disappeared over a six weeks period.

She continued visiting the doctors who prescribed powerful painkillers for her headaches. Over the years the pain worsened. It was difficult for her to concentrate and do her school assignments. She struggled through it and finally graduated from high school, even though we were told that it would not be possible. I was informed by her doctor that she will not be able to go on to higher education because of the severity of her headaches. I maintained my beliefs:

> *For with God nothing shall be impossible. (Luke 1:37)*

The Dade County Youth fair had just opened, and we all descended on it. We were all happy to be out together away from the hospital and the doctors. Ann jumped on the Ferris wheel while the others hopped for the roller coaster. It was about midway in the ride when the operator had to stop the Ferris wheel. I heard a terrifying screaming and I recognized the voice. She had to be taken off confused and bewildered. The scream lasted for a while longer. As soon as we managed to calm her down, she explained the terrifying moment. She stated that she had relived the entire drowning incident and that she was crying out for us to help her. There was some disruption but people were sympathetic towards her. Due to this incident we were always alert around water and rides. After years of fear and caution she went back into the ocean. A mother's ear is attuned to their child's cry. As a child growing up in Jamaica we would always say to someone who annoys you *if I hit you your mother will feel it.* There may be some truth to it; I know I was in constant pain.

"Mom I need a year off from school because I can't start college right now." Ann gave numerous reasons for her decision. I understood her concerns base on her medical condition. Her conception was miraculous and I had no intention for us to be defeated. My reply was, "Ann, do you have an apartment, and a job?" She was stunned by my reply knowing that we provided for our family. I gave her several reasons such as: I will not support an idler. Select one or two courses that you can manage and start college, God will not lead you to fail. I do not believe in failure, there will be setbacks in our lives but we must get up and move on. This chorus inspires me:

Jesus never fails
Jesus never fails
Heaven and Earth shall pass away
But Jesus never fails

Reluctantly, Ann started attending Miami-Dade Community College. She struggled for a while but we supported and cheered her on. She became so engaged that after completing her degree she transferred and continued her studies at Nova Southern University and there she was awarded a Bachelor's and Master's Degree in Education. Shortly afterward she gained employment in a public school. With Ann graduating from high school and from college with two degrees, this was another miracle in our lives.

This entire trauma took a toll on me. It happens that I had to visit a neurologist at Baptist Hospital because of my frequent headaches; I was so moved by the way he attended to me. He used very simple approaches and they worked. Sometime later it dawned on me to tell Ann about him. She quickly made her appointment. We went together and he listened for a very long time intently about the accident and all what transpired. He asked Ann to stand up and he turned her neck in different directions. I heard a pop, I was astonished by the unexpected sound that came from her neck. The doctor explained that he replaced her neck in its original place. Her neck was off the base and this was the reason for the constant headache and fatigue. She came home a new person and has done excellent since.

As the years went by I watched my daughter grow and develop into a successful professional and mother. She has beaten all odds and has given a new meaning to life. I have shared this story with many people especially those who are experiencing trials and tribulations in their lives. It is rewarding to acknowledge God's love and declare His power as Paul did.

> *Now to him who is able to do exceedingly abundantly*
> *above all that we ask or think, according to the power*
> *that works in us, (Ephesians 3:20)*

Our daughter Ann, 2012.

Chapter 8
A Miraculous Healing

Faith is the victory! Faith is the victory!

I can recommend my God to anyone, is Matthew's favorite quote at any given time. He regularly sings or hums this hymn no matter what is in progress. Matthew's day generally begins with his favorite hymn.

O Lord my God, when I in awesome wonder

O Lord my God, when I in awesome wonder
consider all the works thy hand hath made,
I've seen the stars, I hear the mighty thunder,
thy power throughout the universe displayed:

Then sings my soul, my Savior God; to thee,
How great thou art, how great thou art!
Then sings my soul, my Savior God; to thee,
How great thou art, how great thou art!

When through the woods and forest glades I wander,
and hear the birds sing sweetly in the trees;
when I look down from lofty mountain grandeur,
and hear the brook, and feel the gentle breeze;

But when I think that God, his Son not sparing,
sent him to die-I scarce can take it in
that on the cross, our burden gladly bearing,
he bled and died to take away our sin;

It was a warm and peaceful day in summer when I started my usual day. It was unusual for Matthew to be late for work. He took pride in his construction job and being punctual was a ritual for him. This was his source of income and he loved doing his skills. As an experienced mason and carpenter this morning was unusual for him. He woke up late but desperate to share a strange dream that he had. As he got dressed he announced that he did not feel like going to work. I plead for him not to go. "I can't do that," he replied, "I have never done that before and my boss should have been informed much earlier." It was evident that he put his principles above his feelings. Nothing I said or did could have changed his mind. He gave his usual kiss and departed for work. My three children noticed that I was absent- minded, "Mommy are you ok?"

"Why would you think otherwise," I quickly responded.

"You don't act like yourself; you are very quiet this morning." I assured them that I was fine.

As I rode to work my mind wandered; I kept thinking of this strange vision and his determination to please his boss. I took comfort in thinking that he was not sick, so he may have been right. On arrival at work, I quickly engulfed myself in my class activities and quickly forgot all the doubts that I had. Sometime after lunch I was called to the office to receive an emergency message from my son. This was rather strange as he was at home with his older sister. "Hi Mom, a man called and he said that he was Dad's co-worker. He said Dad fell from the overpass and he was taken to Jackson Hospital and you need to go there as quickly as possible." I hurled numerous questions at my eleven year old son, but he was unable to response because he was unaware of the circumstances. I heard the frustration in his voce so I thanked him and assured him that I would go to the hospital immediately and I would call after I got there.

The information was limited and I was so anxious to know if he was dead or alive. I was devastated. I had to move fast in relocating my class as well as all my responsibilities. The news circulated quickly and everyone wanted some kind of explanation but I was not able to help. I informed my boss of the emergency and left in a panic. I quickly reminded myself that I must turn to God's word for comfort. Fear welled up in me.

For God hath not given us the spirit of fear; but of power, and of love, and of a sound mind. (2 Timothy 1:7)

The Lord is my light and my salvation; whom shall I fear? The Lord is the strength of my life; of whom shall I be afraid. (Psalm 27:1)

My heart pounded fast as I drove off to the hospital. I began to pray, "Lord whatever is the situation, please save Matthew's life and keep me very calm so that I can deal with this problem." My thoughts drifted. What if my husband is dead; how would I take care of three young children on my own? I had no family in Miami to assist me. It became so vivid that I would be a widow, a single mother with no finances to support a family. At this point I needed some strength; I turned to my favorite song and I sang it as never before. My inner being was fully consumed by the words and I felt a spiritual connection that made me prepared to face the unknown.

> *When pangs of death seized on my soul,*
> *Unto the Lord I cried;*
> *Till Jesus came and made me whole,*
> *I would not be denied.*
>
> *I would not be denied,*
> *I would not be denied,*
> *Till Jesus came and made me whole,*
> *I would not be denied.*
>
> *As Jacob in the days of old,*
> *I wrestled with the Lord;*
> *And instant, with a courage bold,*
> *I stood upon His Word.*
>
> *Old Satan said my Lord was gone*
> *And would not hear my prayer;*
> *But praise the Lord, the work is done,*
> *And Christ the Lord is here.*

A peace came over me and I suddenly was prepared to face the storm. I felt a surge of strength after singing my favorite hymn. It was just after one o'clock when I arrived, I quickened my strides into Jackson Memorial Hospital Emergency Room. I was directed to the room where he was being examined. As I approached cautiously the security guard prohibited me from entering the room where my husband was placed due to the nature of his injuries. I was polite in informing him who I was and why I was there but he was unwilling to change his orders. I protested, "I am his wife for the past 23 years and he is all that I have, and if I am not allowed to see him then you will go inside and bring him to me in whatever state he is in."

At this point the guard realized that I was not going to take no for an answer. I was determined and prepared to receive him dead or alive. The security guard peered at me as if he had seen a ghost; it appeared as if he was in a state of confusion but remain resolute. Within five minutes I reminded him that I was waiting. "Just bring him out here to me!" He frowned and reluctantly opened the door and escorted me to Matthew. What a sight, I hardly could recognize him. My husband's appearance was shocking, it seemed like a wild beast had mauled him. His clothes were tattered, concrete and dirt had covered his entire body as if he was buried alive. I also noticed that he was wearing an oversized brace on his neck. He was stretched out and strapped down on a broad piece of hard board. He appeared motionless. The sight of him sent shock waves throughout my body; I called out, "Matthew! Matthew!" He slowly opened his eyes. His eyes were extremely red, it appeared like the blood vessels were broken and they were bleeding. There was no way of knowing the extent of his injuries but tears were running from his eyes. What has happened to you Matt? His response seemed to be blank stares. I knew that he was in severe pain and that he had sustained major inquires. The sight of him was enough for me to know that our life was about to take a major turn of events. At that moment I heard the medical team making plans to remove him into a traction bed. This bed is supposed to turn constantly so that his blood can circulate freely. I feared that he may die before morning; I could only mumble from my heart:

> *The LORD is my shepherd; I shall not want.*
> *He maketh me to lie down in green pastures:*
> *He leadeth me beside the still waters. He restoreth my soul:*
> *He leadeth me in the paths of righteousness for his name's sake.*
> *Yea, though I walk through the valley of the shadow of death,*
> *I will fear no evil: for thou art with me; thy rod and thy staff they*
> *comfort me.*
> *Thou preparest a table before me in the presence of mine enemies:*
> *Tthou anointest my head with oil; my cup runneth over.*
> *Surely goodness and mercy shall follow me all the days of my life: and*
> *I will dwell in the house of the LORD forever. (Psalm 23)*

I immediately sought answers from his doctors concerning the extent of his injuries, his present condition, and his prognosis. The outlook was very grim but, I knew how to pray and I also knew God was in control. I was informed that Matthew was unconscious when he arrived at the hospital but he was revived in the hospital. He sustained head trauma, back injuries, knee fractures, along with several other injuries. He was not expected to walk again. It is difficult to be faced with this serious medical dilemma and still give praises unto God. This accident was more reason to praise Him, knowing that his life was spared. I refused to be paralyzed by fear because:

The Joy of the Lord is My Strength. (Nehemiah 8:10)

Being entrusted with my three young children, a full time job, a full college load and the daily visit to the hospital was an extreme task. I juggled from one task to the other and maintained my daily hospital visits. I made it mandatory to review and question all procedures, medication, and therapy that were prescribed, as well as his general condition. The children and I continued to maintain a daily prayer life asking God for Matthew's healing. The medical team was baffled by his miraculous turn-around. Although he had an uncertain road ahead of him we were happy when he was transported home. The living room was transformed into a bedroom to meet some of his medical needs. A medical bed was set up along with other necessities. He wore a hard body brace and knee brace. His excruciating pain put major limitations on his mobility. Daily therapy followed and it was extremely difficult for him to scramble on a walker downstairs to get in my small car. Having experienced Christ's healing power I knew that He would do it again, although I didn't know how or when. I had to keep waiting and trusting Him.

The months that followed were overwhelming trying to get him to the numerous doctors' appointments. On my way to work I dropped the children at school and him at Doctors Hospital for therapy. I would leave work before lunch and struggle with him back home. I had to place all his food, amenities, and medication close to his bedside and hope that he would manage on his own. While the children were on summer break they assisted him as much as possible. Matthew's illness taught me that it is important to have a strong advocate on your side while you are sick. He had surgery, attended pain clinics, and even when things seem bleak his recovery was shocking to others especially his doctors. Although there were bleak moments I encouraged myself in this meditation:

Jesus, Savior, pilot me
Over life's tempestuous sea;
Unknown waves before me roll,
Hiding rock and treacherous shoal.
Chart and compass come from Thee;
Jesus, Savior, pilot me.

His faith and his determination took over and he fought hard to gain strength. Within a year I discovered that he had lost some of his humor. His demeanor had changed and his outlook on life seemed to have changed. With all the medications, illness, as well as our financial situation, he was daunted by the lack of independence and not being able to fully provide for his family. Although his aim was to return to work, he had too many medical problems that prevented him from working. Being injured as well as unemployed presented some major challenges for him. He took pride in knowing that he was the provider and priest of his household. I encouraged him to do alternative things, such as taking music lessons. He did it for a short while but it brought very little comfort to him. We were so grateful to see some improvements knowing that he was not expected to live and that he beats all odds. He was never angry, he kept singing his favorites hymns and continued being thankful and prayerful.

> *Pass me not, O gentle Savior,*
> *Hear my humble cry;*
> *While on others Thou art calling,*
> *Do not pass me by.*
>
> *Savior, Savior,*
> *Hear my humble cry;*
> *While on others Thou art calling,*
> *Do not pass me by.*

Although his pain was agonizing; the treatments seemed never ending, he managed to survive through the goodness and mercies of the Lord. He continued his weekly visits to several doctors and I knew it took a toll on him. He did all he could for the family to maintain a normal life. This journey was really difficult but through the years he has he made a rapid recovery. Through it all we have learned to praise Him.

> *I will bless the LORD at all times: his praise shall continually be in my mouth. My soul shall make her boast in the LORD: the humble shall hear thereof, and be glad. O magnify the LORD with me, and let us exalt his name together. I sought the LORD, and he heard me, and delivered me from all my fears. (Psalm 34:1-4)*

During his time of recovery, our oldest daughter was now a teenager in high school. She complained to us of being harassed constantly by a boy within the community. Matthew decided that we should go along with our daughter together and speak to his parents. Although we did not know him nor were we acquainted with his parents, we thought that this would be the best resolution for this matter. This was a major mistake. On arrival we were greeted by his mother, who welcomed us. Matthew presented the problem and requested that this behavior be stopped. She promised that she would address it immediately. At that point we were about to leave when the mom called her son to meet us. Without warning he emerged with a large shotgun and pointed it directly at us. As I stared at the gun, time stood still. Matthew sprang into action by pushing us behind him and stared at him and shouted three times, "In the name of Jesus dropped your gun!"

There was no time to think, death was imminent for all three of us. His mom screamed at him, "No! No!" Matthew stood firm while I held on to my daughter. In a short while the storm subsided, he went back in his house and we hurried to the police station. Living in a small town like the City of South Miami the Police Chief along with his deputies knew the citizens and their families. The Police Chief escorted him to the station without any incident. He was arrested for attempted murder with a deadly weapon along with other charges. We were much shaken but this was another miracle from God. He was our protector and shield and this is the chorus of deliverance.

The Holy Ghost power is moving just like a magnet
The Holy Ghost power is moving just like a magnet
For it's moving you and it's moving me
Just like the day of Pentecost
The Holy Ghost power is moving just like a magnet
&
Hide me under the blood Lord
Hide me under the blood
And I shall be satisfied

&
He never failed me yet, he never failed me yet
Jesus Christ never failed me yet
Anywhere I go
I want the world to know
Jesus Christ never failed me yet

We did not attend the trial and we had no involvement with the court. Second, we had no idea of how the judicial system worked in the United States. A few times we were contacted by the court to see what our wishes were as it related to sentencing him. The sentence was fully explained which meant going to jail for many years or taking a plea deal. We requested that he be mentally evaluated and be rehabilitated. Our request was honored and he was sentenced to a very long probation, community service, and a no contact with our family. He should not approach within several feet of our dwelling. The court informed us of his sentence and if he failed to abide he would serve a long prison sentence for attempted murder with a deadly weapon. He has kept his distance during these past 20 years. I thank God for his promises.

I will never leave you nor forsake you. (Hebrew 13:5)

Years went by and Matthew took comfort in serving the Lord, tending his plants, which is his passion, and enjoying his family. As an ordained Minister of the Gospel he was scheduled to preach one Sunday morning in 2006. Everything seemed normal as the service progressed; our Bishop introduced him as the morning speaker. The text and message was normal but towards the end there were several repetitions that signaled his departure from this life. "If I don't see you again, please meet me over by River Jordan." Why is he saying this so many times; is something wrong, is he saying his last farewell before going to Heaven? Immediately after dismissal, I got to him. I started to question him about the things that were in the car. I asked him to identify the fruits but he kept looking at them in a strange manner, he appeared confused. What is your name? I enquired, but he still seemed confused. I rushed him to the nearest fire station not knowing what was happening. While I was worried about his health, his concern was if he had preached a good message.

The Emergency Medical Technician (EMT), checked his vitals and stated that did not find anything alarming, but I knew something was wrong, so I rushed him to South Miami Hospital. The hospital was informed that I was on my way. A team of doctors was waiting before I arrived. The doctors tested him for different ailments: stroke, heart attack, as well as other diseases. Matthew enquired why he was there, who the people were that are around him. After about two to three hours of testing, the neurologist informed me of his prognosis. He relayed it in layman's terms, "Your husband's blood ceased flowing for about a second, everything is erased from his memory and he will retain full function within twelve hours. He needs no medication but we will admit him until he recovers." What took place is just like stopping a recorder and starting it again. There are no medical or scientific reasons why this happened. We were all baffled. Matthew's room was flooded with friends, believers, and the hospital staff, who said that they were there to meet the miracle man. We welcomed all the visitors.

> *For I am not ashamed of the gospel, because it is the*
> *power of God unto salvation to everyone who believeth.*
> *(Romans 1:16)*

Matthew became frustrated after seeing so many people around him and he was unable to process what was going on at the hospital and the reason why he was there. He kept repeating the same question, "V why did you take me here?" Although, I explained to him what was taking place several times, he just could not grasp it; finally he went to sleep. *The family huddled together throughout the night and waited.* Monday morning, exactly twelve hours later he awoke singing:

> *I sing because I'm happy*
> *I sing because I'm free*
> *His eye is on the sparrow*
> *And I know He watches me*
> *&*
> *I need Thee, O I need Thee;*
> *Every hour I need Thee;*
> *O bless me now, my Savior,*
> *I come to Thee.*
> *&*
> *There's not a Friend like the lowly Jesus:*
> *No, not one! No, not one!*
> *None else could heal all our souls' diseases:*
> *No, not one! No, not one!*
>
> *Jesus knows all about our struggles;*
> *He will guide 'til the day is done:*
> *There's not a Friend like the lowly Jesus:*
> *No, not one! No, not one!*
>
> *No friend like Him is so high and holy,*

No, not one! No, not one!
And yet no friend is so meek and lowly,
No, not one! No, not one!

There's not an hour that He is not near us,
No, not one! No, not one!
No night so dark, but His love can cheer us,
No, not one! No, not one!

Many of the staff and onlookers were amazed, some joined in the celebration. God answers prayer. He was too happy to keep quiet.

While I was busy seeking explanations from the doctors and trying to understand this unusual medical occurrence our spiritual leader along with others were praying for his recovery. The focus was on God's deliverance and help. As they prayed I was confident that God would heal him;

God can do anything but fail.

He was fully aware of his environment and wanted a full account of the circumstances that brought him there. He took another round of testing before permission was granted for him to leave the hospital. We had a long discussion with him until he was discharged later that morning. Our only explanation of this incident is that this must be a miracle. My husband walked out of South Miami Hospital without being medicated, fully functional, and we all praise God for His healing.

I will lift up mine eyes unto the hills, from whence
cometh my help. My help cometh from the Lord which
made heaven and earth. (Psalm 121:1-2)

I knew that God has delivered us one more time, and this is why I communed with Him.

Praise. him, praise him
Praise him in the morning
Praise him in the evening
Praise him, praise him
Praise him when the sun goes down

Looking back over these circumstances and the victory won; I knew that it was God's supernatural power that had propelled us this far. We could not have succeeded through these storms on our own. I remain grateful to God for all these miracles that occurred in my life. The song sums it up.

What a friend we have in Jesus,
all our sins and griefs to bear!
What a privilege to carry everything to God in prayer!

O what peace we often forfeit, O what needless pain we bear, all because we
do not carry everything to God in prayer

Have we trials and temptations? Is there trouble anywhere?
We should never be discouraged; take it to the Lord in prayer.
Can we find a friend so faithful who will all our sorrows share?

Jesus knows our every weakness; take it to the Lord in prayer.
Are we weak and heavy laden, cumbered with a load of care?
Precious Savior, still our refuge; take it to the Lord in prayer.

Do thy friends despise, forsake thee? Take it to the Lord in prayer!
In his arms he'll take and shield thee; thou wilt find a solace there.

Our family, 2004.

Chapter 9
Unknown Territory- Eight Years in Politics

*Thou wilt keep him in perfect peace, whose mind is stayed
on thee: because he trusted in thee. (Isaiah 26:3)*

Isaiah's song of Gods praise and protection kept me throughout these
slippery slopes that could have cost me my very existence. Someone once
said that the greatest thing in life is to know. It was evident that I did
not know how government functioned. It was the summer of 1993 and
I was frustrated with South Miami's City Government for not providing
assistance to the needy, so I visited City Hall and demanded stationery to
use in my effort to help the residents. It was customary for me to write to
different agencies in order to assist the less fortunate in an effort to move
their lives forward. I was serving on the Community Action Agency
Advisory Board that put me in direct contact with people and their needs.
I was new but vibrant and strove for the best.

I had no idea that I would enter politics that very moment I set foot on
their ground. I entered two offices and was surprised that my request was
unheard of; I strolled outside with a sense of disappointment and feeling
defeated. As I left the office, I greeted two men whom I knew. I wasted no
time in laying my burden on them. They assured me that city government
did not function the way we thought it should, they do not provide the
kind of assistance that I was seeking for the residents. We started to discuss
community activities and one of the men informed me that there would
be an election in fifteen months. They also relayed that I would be a good
candidate. My immediate response was that they should consider running
for the commission seats. However, both declined for different reasons. I
felt 'cornered' as they both suggested that I would be the ideal candidate.
"No, No," I protested, "I have no idea or experience to do that job." You
are the person to be our commissioner the older gentleman implored. I was
confused and baffled by this encounter. Why would they even suggest this
with so much confidence? I struggled with the thought and was unable
to remove it from my mind. I kept thinking about it for days but I could

not comprehend the incident. I was unaware at the time that I had been assigned to go on the battlefield.

> *Therefore take unto you the whole armor of God, that*
> *you may be able to withstand in the evil day, and having*
> *done all, to stand. (Ephesians 6:13)*

I knew someone who would agree with me and this would end the battle in my mind. I was so sure that my decision would be supported by others that I called three ministers and a friend who were close to me and to my surprise they were all in favor of me running for a commission seat in the City of South Miami. I was determined to have someone to support my decision so I ended up with four calls. My husband's reaction was beyond my expectation, "I will support you, you should try it," he stated. Now, I was trapped, so I reluctantly enquired in the city clerk's office about the process. She handed me a package and gave me some simple directions. It seemed quite easy as she outlined the instructions. I did not realize what was awaiting me.

After accomplishing the first two steps, thinking the task was almost completed, I came to her for directions. "Now that you have completed your paper work you must go around and knock on ten thousand doors and explain to them who you are, and then seek their vote." Did I hear this woman correctly? "What! No, I have changed my mind!" She just smiled, and in a soft encouraging voice, "Yes you can do it."

> *Thus says the LORD unto you, Be not afraid nor*
> *dismayed by reason of this great multitude; for the battle*
> *is not yours, but God's. (2 Chronicles 20:15)*

Mrs. Moore my friend and Matthew did not hesitate, "Let's start walking tomorrow." We began, and after a short time others joined in although we did not know anything about running a campaign. Mrs. Moore became the campaign manager in her own way. My children assisted me in preparing the campaign literature on my computer at home. This went on for months until I collected some donations and upgraded the campaign literature. My daily message to the voters for one year was: *My name is Velma Palmer and I am a teacher for more than 25 years. I do not have anything to give to you but I will be your voice and represent you to the best of my ability. I will appreciate you voting for me so that I can be your commissioner.*

The residents received me with open arms. They expressed their feelings; they wanted their representative to be fearless, honest and fair. My motto throughout the campaign was, "If I can help somebody as I passed along then my living will not be in vain." At first, I was not convinced this was an assignment from God. I was unsure of the path to take and my daily thoughts were consumed with questions of my purpose. Why would God want me to do this? I took courage as I looked over the lives of others and how He has protected them.

I press toward the mark for the prize of the high calling
of God in Christ Jesus. (Philippians 3:14)

My prayers were later answered when I was elected. My triumph in all the precincts was remarkable; I won the election and was sworn in office as the Vice Mayor of the City of South Miami. This was the first time I voted in the United States of America and I voted for myself. I had gotten my citizenship less than three years prior to this historic event. Some people were convinced that I could not win because I was born and raised in the Caribbean but that did not impede my progress. Most people wanted a strong leader and they observed that in me.

The steps of a good man are ordered by the Lord, And
He delights in his way. Though he fall, he shall not be
utterly cast down;For the Lord upholds him with His
hand. (Psalm 37:23-24)

I knew all along that with God all things are possible. I needed only to believe. I am convinced that God has brought people in my path for special reasons. I met and became friends with Cathy McCann an accomplished woman who had served the City of South Miami as a Mayor, Vice Mayor and Commissioner for 16 years. We were both strong-willed women but we respected each other's boundaries and did not take anything for granted. We established a great friendship and this was the one person I trusted to share my thoughts and opinion. She was well versed in legal matters, ordinances, Roberts Rules of Order, and the City Charter. Her support was valuable and we kept close. I quickly realized that I was naïve. I was convinced that I would sit with the Mayor and Commissioners and work on programs and solve problems in the best interest of the citizen. I was totally wrong. It dawned on me that I was now in a lion's den and I could be eaten alive. My assertiveness was a bit unusual in this business compounded with my no-nonsense approach, which only added fuel to the fire.

"What did I get myself into?" Alli, my youngest daughter refreshed my memory, "Mummy, you always prayed and asked God to allow you to be of help to people. You were not specific as to what you wanted to do so this is what you have gotten. This is a way of helping people. Next time tell God exactly what you mean." Although, I muttered to myself that she was right; I was not willing to admit it openly.

> *Fear thou not; for I am with thee: be not dismayed; for I am thy God: I will strengthen thee; yea, I will help thee; yea, I will uphold thee with the right hand of my righteousness. (Isaiah 41:10)*

Vice Mayor Velma Palmer, 2004.

Politics

Cathy and I would meet sometimes, but there were times when there was urgency in her call. After lengthy discussions and reviewing documents I was convinced that she wanted me to continue her legacy. One day I said, "It seems like you want to turn me into Cathy McCain." She laughed convincingly. She constantly shared her knowledge about government with me, explaining complicated processes while allowing me to grow on my own.

After four years I was re-elected and she was ecstatic. Early in my second term as a commissioner Cathy became very ill. We met and discussed her illness and we cried and prayed together knowing that her departure was at hand. Her favorite question to me was, "Are you praying hard enough for me? Velma you must remain strong and don't forget to carry on my legacy of affordable housing. There is more, you must sing *when the saints go marching in* at my funeral." I knew that this would be our farewell. Our friendship was special and I am convinced that God brought her in my life for a special reason. I learned a lot and I will always cherish that chapter in my life.

The last thing I did to convey my appreciation to her family and to cherish Cathy's memory was to spearhead the renaming of 58th Avenue to Cathy McCann Drive. The naming ceremony was conducted at the Dante Fascell Park adjacent to the now renamed Cathy McCann Drive. My determination to accomplish that goal for her was well received by her family, friends, and the community. We came together and celebrated her life at the opening of her street.

I am reminded of a scripture that says God will not take me to a darker path than he has trod. This is a path that lends itself to the unknown world. My thoughts and experiences led me to believe that politics are just like a maze. Years ago, as a child I visited a botanical garden in Jamaica and it kept me on my feet. I was determined not to get lost in the maze because all the areas looked alike so I carefully noticed every step I took. Similarly, I could not allow myself to get lost or swallowed up by politics so I trod carefully not taking anything for granted. My survival on the dais was contained in this song.

Leaning, leaning, safe and secure from all alarms;
Leaning, leaning, leaning on the everlasting arms.

What have I to dread, what have I to fear,

Leaning on the everlasting arms;
I have blessed peace with my Lord so near,
Leaning on the everlasting arms.

Leaning, leaning, safe and secure from all alarms;
Leaning, leaning, leaning on the everlasting arms.

I had to lean on Jesus daily because danger was always present while in government. Being in this position while maintaining my career and my family was extremely challenging, but I am also grateful for the experience. I was able to impact the community in a positive manner with the decisions that I have made. Although there was turmoil, in many situations during my last two years at City Hall, I was at peace and able to withstand the tide. There is always a storm before the calm and this was during the change of guards. I made it public that it states in the Book of Psalms that

The angel of the Lord encamped around them that fear
him, and delivered them. (Psalm 34:7)

My survival rested on one thing only and that was Christ. In this position I understood what David was saying:

They that trust in the LORD shall be as mount Zion,
which cannot be removed, but abideth for ever. (Psalm
125:1)

This is real and cannot be seen with the natural eyes. I have encountered some devious characters whose only aim was destruction. The Holy Spirit opened my eyes constantly to the traps that were carefully planted while the enemy waited in disguise for my demise. A spiritual barricade kept all negative forces at bay. There were times on the dais that I had spiritual revelations made known to me and the Holy Spirit for my protection gave them all to me. I was told by some of my colleagues that no one ever seemed to understand me. The reason being I followed the Lord's instructions and it confused the schemers. Second, I was a straight shooter who was not influenced by anyone, their gifts, or any circumstances. I prayed for direction and guidance and that was what influenced the decisions that I made. This is why I was able to sing with confidence:

Jesus builds a fence, all around me everyday
Lord I want you to protect me as I journey along life's way

> *Lord I know you will, Lord I know you can*
> *Fight my battles while I just keep still*
> *Build a fence all around me everyday*

This reminded me of the warning my grandmother gave me especially when I am leaving the home "keep your eyes open at all times." She meant that I should be alert and watchful at all times of others. My upbringing and the Christian training and commitment to the Lord had really laid a major foundation for this difficult task.

During my eight years in government my approach to any matter was open, truthful and fair. When I reviewed the way I voted, I took steps to make corrections if it were deemed necessary. I had made amendments to decisions if new information came to light; I was not afraid to do the right thing. My motto stayed with me, because I knew my purpose and cause. My style was considered the first in the city and it was puzzling to many people while the majority thanked me.

Politics is a difficult job and anyone who wishes to serve should not take it lightly or else they will be devoured. A situation arose that was intended for my demise and I had to announce to my colleagues that:

> *No weapon that is formed against thee shall prosper;*
> *and every tongue that shall rise against thee in judgment*
> *thou shalt condemn. This is the heritage of the servants*
> *of the LORD, and their righteousness is of me, saith the*
> *LORD. (Isaiah 54:17)*

I made my announcement of my departure in January of 2012 at one of our regular commission meetings. In my speech I mentioned that serving in government was never my intent but God directed me to this position. My younger daughter always reminds me that when you make a request unto God you must be specific. My request was to serve people; I was not specific in my prayer request. I thanked everyone for their years of support and encouraged them to do their part in supporting our city. The line that was most telling was that I told God to let me serve the city in an honorable way, and leave in a respectful manner; just like the way I came. Until now I have remained clean. It was a touching speech for the entire city because numerous people urged me to continue to serve. The thanks were overwhelming, but I knew it was time for me to go. The room was full of laughter when I said, "Eight is enough!" I thanked God for His grace and I left *The City of Pleasant Living* gracefully. I will cherish these memories. I rested my hope in these great songs:

Where He may leads me I will go
For I have learned to trust him so
He is the truest Friend to me,
For I remember Calvary.

Jesus shall lead me night and day,
Jesus shall lead me all the way,
He is the truest Friend to me,
For I remember Calvary.
&
Closer than a brother Jesus is to me
He's my dearest friend He's everything I need
He's my rock, my shield and hiding place
Closer than a brother Jesus is to me

Chapter 10
Walk With God

>

*For I know the thoughts that I think towards you, saith the Lord,
thoughts of peace, and not of evil, to give you an expected end.
Then shall ye call upon me, and ye shall go and pray unto me, and
I will hearken unto you. And ye shall seek me, and find me, when
ye shall search for me with all your heart. (Jeremiah 29:11-13)*

My prosperity is not dependent on material things only but it is mainly spiritual gifts that are priceless. I am unable to express the level of gratitude that is in my heart for Christ's love and His grace that he bestowed upon me. It is my delight to share these experiences of faith with you. While writing this book, I realized that some of the events triggered both joyful and painful memories. I have tried my best to show how God has not only guided me but how He has always held my hand through each and every tribulation. God's love towards me has been poured out in abundance of blessings in the form of talents, intelligence, understanding, knowledge, energy, opportunities, relationships, and resources. God has afforded me these benefits that are beyond my description as well as my comprehension. Most of all he has empowered me with the gift of the Holy Spirit who protects, guides, and keeps me daily. I am deeply grateful for His investment in me. Sometimes the measure of my gratitude can only be expressed in affirmation, and songs. While viewing my years of victories my inner being rejoices in singing:

*I have found a friend in Jesus, He's everything to me,
He's the fairest of ten thousand to my soul;
The Lily of the Valley, in Him alone I see
All I need to cleanse and make me fully whole.
In sorrow He's my comfort, in trouble He's my stay;
He tells me every care on Him to roll.*

*He's the Lily of the Valley, the Bright and Morning Star,
He's the fairest of ten thousand to my soul.*

He all my grief has taken, and all my sorrows borne;
In temptation He's my strong and mighty tower;
I have all for Him forsaken, and all my idols torn
From my heart and now He keeps me by His power.
Though all the world forsake me, and Satan tempt me sore,
Through Jesus I shall safely reach the goal.
He's the Lily of the Valley, the Bright and Morning Star,
He's the fairest of ten thousand to my soul.

As a teenager, I was fearful of the new life that would begin after I surrendered my life to Christ. Even before I asked, He has provided for my family and me, a lot more that I could have asked for. Despite the many challenges that Matthew and I endured, we managed to overcome them. Even now after 44 years of marriage Matthew's compliments remain constant, "I love your unique qualities especially your assertiveness." Christ has given me a boldness to combat my fearfulness of challenges or people's negative actions. For years, I was inspired to write this book but I was bogged down with numerous responsibilities but God kept reminding me that I should write. I was unable to escape His urging, until it became a weight, so I obeyed but not without some sacrifices. I selected my own title when I began, but I heard a voice speaking to me distinctly--the title of the book is *Untold Miracles*. I started to think about it for a while and then I complied. At times I stopped writing but there was His voice again--just like in this chapter.

I hope that sharing my experiences about God's favors and miracles will inspire you to worship Jesus Christ with your whole heart. My encouragement and testimony have led many people to activate their gifts; some have committed their lives to the Lord, others went back to school and achieved their goal. I have made myself available for those who are hurting, discouraged, and misguided; sometimes they just need my listening ear, a smile or a hug. One of God's purposes for my life is spelled out in this song.

Rescue the perishing, care for the dying,
Snatch them in pity from sin and the grave;
Weep o'er the erring one, lift up the fallen,
Tell them of Jesus, the mighty to save

Down in the human heart, crushed by the tempter,
Feelings lie buried that grace can restore;

> *Touched by a loving heart, wakened by kindness,*
> *Chords that were broken will vibrate once more.*

While my children were growing they always wondered why people always wanted their Mummy to listen to their problems and find solutions; they did not understand my purpose in this life. Mama always reminded me, "Betty, do all the good you can, God's goodness and mercy will follow you all the days of your life." There were days when I was confronted with problems that were beyond my comprehension. I sought the Lord on their behalf, and we rejoiced when the victory was won. I am known to share my blessings constantly with others. I do not complain about money because God holds the wealth of the world in His hands. I am His child and He gave me a promise.

> *Behold the fowls of the air: for they sow not, neither*
> *do they reap, nor gather into barns; yet your heavenly*
> *Father feedeth them. Are ye not much better than they?*
> *(Matthew 6:26)*

One summer, I ran out of money and I looked up to Heaven, I spoke to the Lord in a few words, "Lord you said that the cattle on the hills are yours, you may need to sell some of them because the bills are due and I am unable to pay them." Within days two checks arrived in the mail, it was a bit strange to us: Matthew was refunded $4,000 for overpayment on his life insurance policy. The second check which was much less came from my annuity retirement fund due to a mistake that was made and it was too late to credit it to the account. I have known Christ Jesus as a provider, a healer, an emancipator, a comforter, a protector, a leader, a friend among other things. I will always embrace the opportunities that God has afforded me.

I cannot forget my humble beginnings, in rural Jamaica where there were no running water in my home, no sewage system, long walks on rocky roads to and from schools, limited transportation system, no electricity, no gas stoves or refrigerator, and we had to plant and harvest our own crops. Although people in the cities had these comforts, I was very happy in my rural area because we were healthy and blessed. Honestly, I believe that God has blessed me with a happy family, a modern and spacious home along with all the modern amenities that provided comfort for me, my family, and the people who visit us. There are times when it is important for me to reflect on my past so I ask the Lord to:

Roll back the curtain of memory now and then
Show me where you brought me from
And where I could have been
Remember I'm human, and humans forget
So remind me, remind me dear Lord

The things that I love and hold dear to my heart
Are just borrowed they're not mine at all
Jesus only let me use them to brighten my light
So remind, me remind me dear Lord

Greatness is in us, we just need to find it, but it will not be on our own terms. I am convinced that God has a purpose for all of us. I make it a point to remain humble knowing that my help cometh from the Lord. He has fought my battles and I receive the victories all because:

Each step I take my Saviour goes before me,
And with His loving hand He leads the way,
And with each breath I whisper "I adore Thee;"
Oh, what joy to walk with Him each day

Each step I take I know that He will guide me;
To higher ground He ever leads me on.
Until some day the last step will be taken.
Each step I take just leads me closer home

Don't misunderstand, I had many setbacks on this journey but they were the major aspects that propelled my growth process in God, and my successes in life. I consider my challenges the force that molds me and keeps me focused, while I gain strength. The obstacles have taught me that I must depend on Jesus for directions and guidance even in the simplest of matters. Although I had people around me who sought to destroy my life in various ways, they have seen their well-planned schemes evaporate and I remained steadfast. I also had great attacks from the enemy on my family's life but through it all we were victorious.

Then shalt thou delight thyself in the LORD; and I will
cause thee to ride upon the high places of the earth, and
feed thee with the heritage of Jacob thy father: for the
mouth of the LORD hath spoken it. (Isaiah 58:14)

Through the Spirit of discernment God has revealed the dangers to us while being our shield and protector in those difficult times. The enemy became so fearful, seeing no alternative they had to flee. This is what David declared in Psalm 91:7-8

> *A thousand shall fall at thy side, and ten thousand at thy right hand; but it shall not come nigh thee. Only with thine eyes shalt thou see and behold the reward of the wicked.*

Many of my friends have enquired, how do you withstand all these difficulties and still stand? In politics, on the job, and even sometimes among believers, I had to stand alone against Goliath using the sword, which is the word of God. My favorite response to them was *not by might, nor by power, but by my spirit of God.*

My grandmother taught me that, "Your mind can make you and it can break you." She encouraged me to have a good mind towards others, so I fostered a keen and sound mind in my daily walk. She suggested that my future prosperity was dependent on these things and I believed and practiced it. I have seen how God has opened so many doors for my family and me. It has been revealed to John the Revelator by God that we should be prosperous and that is why he was able to write these words for the believer in Christ:

> *Beloved, I wish above all things that thou mayest prosper and be in health, even as thy soul prospereth. (3 John 1:3)*

God IS My Provider

Some years ago, I was on the busy expressway and my old car blanketed the area with thick black smoke that amounted to a large amount of air pollution. I was alerted to an empty highway as I traveled; the drivers kept their distance from me. After arriving to my destination I parked and hours later my car refused to start. The director examined the car and pointed out that I had a "she needs a", this meant the car is dead. On arriving at the dealership I tried to select the least expensive used car. Matthew protested, "If you have been serving God all this time and He cannot provide a good car for you then I suggest that you stop serving Him." He sat on a new Chrysler Dynasty; he thought that I deserved it.

"You know we can't afford it," I protested. But he did not reply. The salesman who was unknown to us suggested I take the car home without any commitment for a week to see if I liked it. Sure enough, I returned to the dealership before the allotted time and credited the car by faith. Within two months the Lord provided a new teaching position for me at Miami-Dade County Public School, which gave me a significant raise in salary. He also provided an additional resource that was used to pay off the car within a short time.

Another experience that I want to share with you is the way Christ selected our first home for us here when we could not afford it.

> *Count your blessings, name them one by one,*
> *Count your blessings, see what God hath done!*
> *Count your blessings, name them one by one,*
> *And it will surprise you what the Lord hath done.*

Matthew was recuperating from his accident so I started to design and sell hats to supplement our income. As I filled one of my orders in the City of South Miami, one of my customers approached me and insisted that I inspect a house that was directly in front of hers. I had no interest in seeing it but she was not letting me go without looking at it. "We needed a good neighbor here, I know you would be excellent," she implored. I informed her that she could not make that kind of statement when she really did not know me, but that did not prevent her from holding on to her opinion of me. I reluctantly followed her around as she pointed out every corner of the property. The entire conversation was based on me buying the property; I showed my respect but I was desperate to leave.

During dinner, I mentioned it to Matthew not knowing that he would get excited about it. I told him the only value that I saw was a beautiful expensive door on the house. I could not get any peace because of his constant interrogation concerning the land size. After numerous requests, I finally agreed to take him to see the property, and there we saw the realtor posting a for sale sign. Matthew fell in love with the property due to its size and its location. I dragged my feet for days before agreeing to a small deposit of $500 on this small two-bedroom house. The realtor rushed to find a bank loan for us. I did not pay much attention to the process until someone called from bank with an appointment for us meet with them. My husband was receiving two thirds of his salary from workers compensation due to his injuries so he was not considered employed. I would not be able to qualify on my meager salary.

A week before the meeting with bank, my director at the school where

I worked requested a meeting with me. He increased my salary by $3000 after reviewing my qualifications. I needed the exact increase on my yearly salary to qualify for the mortgage. At the closing of the purchase I was credited for damages and missing items from the home, which reduced the sales price of the home. We came prepared to pay what was agreed on at the closing but no money was collected. I was informed that the bank cannot lend below a certain amount of money and this house price was the exact amount so I was able to keep my cash. We closed on the home with no money down; only the $500 deposit that was made at the beginning was spent. Again, God is my provider! No money was paid down on both items in my time of need. I came to understand the song that Mama taught me as a child. We were so bonded that we would sing it together over and over again. I did not know why she made it a point to start it while we were doing chores together.

Two little children were walking one day
Down by the dark riverside
They were singing and shouting and praising their God
The Lord will provide

Certainly, He has constantly provided for me beyond my needs so I am sharing my life experiences with you because *I am not ashamed of this gospel; it is the power unto salivation.* Every aspect of my life He held in His hands. At times I try to pluck my hands away from Him by doing things my way but He gave me that anchor that kept me safe. I often say, why does he love me so much after all my faults and failures? The answer remains the same, "I love you; I gave my life for you." I endorse David's words in Psalm 34:8:

O taste and see that the LORD is good: blessed is the man
that trusts in him.

He spoke from his experiences with God. I would encourage you to do just that. Invite Him in your life and then you will fully understand the message that is in this book. You are created for a special purpose but you cannot fulfill your purpose until you know what it is. Take time out to ask yourself, "What is God's purpose for my life?" There cannot be happiness and total freedom until we are fulfilling our purpose.

At times, our aspirations become meaningless because they are based on our own principles. We are proud to be served but sometimes unwilling to serve others. Our life is a journey and there is a compass to guide us on this trip. I believe if I follow His guidance I will reach my destination safely even in the worst weather. In my life I have encountered several boisterous storms, overcast and dark skies, gloomy situations, high waves tossing to and fro, but one thing was sure for my survival was:

> *Standing on the promises of God I cannot fail*
> *When the howling storms of doubt and fear assail,*
> *By the living Word of God I shall prevail*
> *I'm standing on the promises of God.*

I must warn you that these were difficult times but I did not have the need to worry because, *My Daddy was at the wheel,* so I was able to sleep. It is very easy to lose your course on this life's journey or to be shipwrecked; we all can be safe if we just let Him hold our hand.

> *As I travel thru this pilgrim land*
> *There is a Friend who walks with me,*
> *Leads me safely thru the sinking sand,*
> *It is the Christ of Calvary;*
> *This would be my pray'r, dear Lord, each day*
> *To help me do the best I can,*
> *For I need Thy light to guide me day and night*
> *Blessed Jesus, hold my hand.*

> *Blessed Jesus, hold my hand,*
> *Yes, I need Thee ev'ry hour,*
> *Thru this land, this pilgrim land*
> *Protect me by Thy saving pow'r;*
> *Hear my plea, my feeble plea,*
> *Lord, dear Lord, look down on me,*
> *When I kneel in prayer,*
> *Blessed Jesus, hold my hand.*

Your circumstances can change any day, so make sure that you know the Rock which is Jesus. I recall a poem that I have learned as a youth by Etienne de Grellet that was written centuries ago and still rings true:

I shall pass this way but once;
Any good that I can do
Or any kindness I can show to any human being;
Let me do it now.
Let me not defer nor neglect it,
For I shall not pass this way again.

Testimony

I have known Dr. Velma Palmer for more than 20 years. We met when we were both teaching preschool in a day care at the Methodist Church in Miami. My first impression of Velma was that she was a formidable woman. Standing nearly six feet tall, she had a raspy Jamaican voice and a no-nonsense approach to things. She also had a calming and gentle spirit. Daily she'd be on the floor laughing and playing with Legos and bristle blocks along with the kids in her class in the day care.

There are few things that rattle Velma. Over the years I have come to know why. Velma Palmer is a woman of God. He is her foundation, her rock. She said to me that she was going to get her degree. "I don't have any money, but God will make a way." Velma got her degree. She said the same thing about her Master's, "I don't have any money, but God will make a way." Velma got her Master's on faith and determination and became a 6th grade teacher, and a city commissioner, while pursing her Doctorate.

It would be remiss not to mention her second rock, Matthew-- her husband, her confidant, and her best friend. He has been by her side and on her side come rain or shine. Like two palms in the breeze, they sway as one.

If any of my other friends told me that they were going to write a book, I would have balked at the idea. However, with Velma's inner strength, God, and her outer strength, Matthew, I have no doubt that Velma will land in the "sea of tranquility."

-Scharmaine Taylor

Bibliography

King James Study Bible, King James Version. (1988), Nashville: Thomas Nelson Publishers, Inc.

Redemption Songs and Choruses. London: Collins Publishers.

Banner Hymns. (1957), Cleveland, Tennessee: White Wing Publishing House.

Acknowledgements

As always, I must start by thanking God for being the Supreme Ruler of my life, who has protected and guided me through my dreams and my entire life. I am also grateful that He has prompted me for years to write this book although I had my personal fears.

I give Him thanks and praise for the way He has empowered me with knowledge, wisdom, and understanding throughout this journey. I am eternally grateful to God the Father, God the Son, and God the Holy Spirit for His daily protection, and provisions.

I am especially thankful for Matthew, my loving husband, friend, and confidant. He has provided endless support for me as I spent numerous hours typing and reflecting on each chapter that sometimes became painful. You are a tower of strength and I will always love you.

My three children, Antoinette, Allison, Ricardo, I am thankful for the motivation, and backing that you had provided for me. You were all able to encourage me when I stopped writing: "You can do it Mom," was the constant urging. May the Lord allow you to find favor in His sight as He continues to bless your lives. I love you.

I would be remiss if I did not acknowledge my spiritual leader Bishop Simeon Downs; special thanks for his support and spiritual guidance to me and my family throughout the years.

The author would like to thank Kerry-Ann Brown who patiently and faithfully read through the draft. Your honest comments are respected and appreciated.

Special thanks for my friends Brandhilda Moore, Scharmine Taylor and my brother Lloyd Brown for their friendship and for their testimonials. Branhilda has been a good friend, and a tower of strength to me in achieving my goal.

Authors Biography

Velma Palmer Ph.D. is the second of eleven children, born and raised in the parish of Saint Mary, Jamaica, West Indies. As a child she attended Donnington All Age School in Saint Mary. She graduated from Warren Hall High School and Mico Teacher's College in Kingston, Jamaica. At the age of fifteen she had surrendered her life to the Lord and has experienced countless miracles filled with endless blessings beyond the ordinary. Her passion and spiritual gifts were revealed at an early age at National Baptist Church of God in Kingston where she taught Sunday school, directed and counseled youth meetings, and served as a Missionary Leader. During the past 40 years she has been an active member of the Church of God of Prophecy both in Jamaica and the United States of America; mainly at Triumphant Church of God of Prophecy in Cutler Bay. As an ordained minister she has served the ministry in various capacities throughout the years. She has been married to Minister Matthew Palmer for 44 years and is the mother of three children and five grand children.

After working as a certified teacher at Greenwich All Age Elementary for thirteen years, she migrated to Miami, Florida in the summer of 1985. She has always been eager to learn and that inspired her to return to college where she was awarded an Associate Degree from Miami-Dade College, a Bachelor's Degree in Elementary Education, and a Master's Degree in Guidance and Counseling from Nova Southeastern University, and a Doctor of Philosophy Degree in Mathematics from Curtin University of Technology. Over the past 35 years her teaching career has impacted thousands of lives at different age levels; she is proud to motivate others to reach their highest potential in life.

Author's Contact Information

Dr. Velma Palmer
Tel: (786) 464-9019 or (786)-208-9718
Email: aspiration302@gmail.com
www.perserverance1.com